Biddenden Murderers

Cane Hills

Copyright © 2022

All rights reserved. No part of this publication may be reproduced, stored in a retrieval system, or transmitted in any form, or by any means, without the prior permission in writing of the publisher.

First printed 2022

ISBN: 9781915424693

Other books written by Cane Hills

Buckingham Joe,

ISBN 978-1-5289223-2-6,

Austin Macauley Publishers, London. 2020.

Contents

About the Author

Cane Hills was born in 1953 and studied at John Ruskin Grammar School, Shirley, Croydon. He started working in data processing in 1970 and continued in this sphere for a third of a century, writing many technical documents during this time. He then moved into the world of stained glass, working predominantly on domestic properties in the London area. *Biddenden Murderers* is his second publication and completes the subject of the nefarious goings-on in Wealden Kent, which was started with *"Buckingham Joe"*.

Introduction

The village of Biddenden lies in the depths of Wealden Kent, about fourteen miles from the ever-expanding conurbation of Ashford. Although many of its inhabitants do commute to and from London on a daily basis, it is predominantly of a rural nature. A population of over two thousand souls reside here, begging the question as to whether it should be referred to as a small town. However, the area still retains its village atmosphere rather proudly with its parish church, village pub and quaint lop-sided antique buildings.

Perhaps Biddenden's main claim to fame is the well-documented tale of the Chulkhurst twins. Elisa and Mary were conjoined twins who were born around the year 1100 and managed to survive for 34 years. Much myth and legend surround their lives and subsequent bequest to the poor of the village, for which a charity still exists to this day.

The Story of Biddenden, published for the Biddenden Local History Society (1996), describes Biddenden as "One of the loveliest villages in the Weald of Kent". Despite its tranquil beauty, it has, on occasion, attracted what can only be described as the wrong sort of person into its community. These include men and women who, for whatever reason, have taken it upon themselves to deprive others of their existence in the most brutal of manners — for these are the Biddenden Murderers.

The following tales are an attempt to record the murders that have taken place within the parish of Biddenden or have been committed by residents of the same between the latter part of the eighteenth century and the present day. They have been gleaned mainly from newspaper articles and, in particular, from provincial organs, which are far more likely to be sympathetic to the local point of view rather than those of the often-over-sensationalised articles sometimes found in columns of our national press.

Cane Hills, 2022

Chapter 1 - Early Murderers

With the exception of Thomas Oliver, there was very little information about the earlier Biddenden murderers in the provincial press of the day. The case of Oliver, who murdered Jonathan May at Moretonhampstead, Devon, in July 1835, was well reported nationally and eventually, it attracted international attention as well. Because of the completeness of the whole saga, it has been fully documented by this author in a separate publication: *Buckingham Joe*. However, it was quite possible that, in this case, the links with Biddenden were false or could be described as, at least, tenuous.

The remaining three cases, all of which pre-dated the activities of Bertha Peterson in 1899, had many similarities with each other. Firstly, the body of the victim was not discovered until sometime after the fatal injuries had been inflicted, by which time the trail was cold. And to make matters worse, the investigative techniques and technology of the day were only capable of determining very limited incriminating evidence from what remained. Secondly, the identities of the victims were never revealed to the public at large, even when they may have been known to the authorities investigating the murders. Finally, the same condition of anonymity was applied with respect to the identity of the perpetrators of the offences, all of whom, it would appear, managed to escape ever being brought to justice. And as to whether any of the incidents were ever followed up by the limited criminal investigators of the day is unknown and highly unlikely.

- - - o o o - - -

The first offence occurred in the summer of 1773 on the outskirts of the village and to the northeast of the parish.

Monday, 21st June 1773

A young woman who belonged to Biddenden was passing through a wood between Biddenden and Smarden on her way to Smarden market to sell some of her master's butter. She was accosted by an unidentified travelling man and woman who stripped her of her clothes. The wretched victim used her last breaths to cry: "Murder!" before she was done to death.

Two men, who were cutting faggots nearby, heard the woman's desperate cries for help and rushed to the wood. On their way there, they encountered the couple carrying a bundle, presumably containing the dead woman's clothes. When asked if they had heard the cry of 'Murder!', the travelling woman immediately replied, "My devilish husband has been beating me so, that I thought he would have killed me."

Saturday, 14th August 1773

More than seven weeks after the crime was committed, the body of the young woman was finally found. The corpse was naked and 'much defaced by vermin'. The night before, and the morning following the discovery, the whole of the south and east of England was subjected to a great deluge of biblical proportions, yet the body was still found despite the conditions it had been through.

Wednesday, 8th September 1773

A report appeared in the *Kentish Gazette* stating that the previous reports of the murderous attack were erroneous and that the scene of the crime was not, as previously reported, in a wood between Biddenden and Smarden, but in Romden Wood, near Wissenden. It also declared that the reported victim was alive and well and employed in haymaking at Brookland, 17 miles to the southeast of Biddenden, near Rye.

Despite an exhaustive and comprehensive search of the provincial press of 1773 (including the entire Burney Collection at the British Library), only two newspaper articles were ever published concerning the details of this case. The first was in mid-August 1773, which reported the discovery of the corpse seven weeks subsequent to its demise, and the second, in early September 1773, which denied the fact of murder and changed the supposed location of the crime.

In the light of these two news stories, it can be presumed that no progress occurred in the apprehension of the culprits and that they remained anonymous and at large. Although the identity of the victim must have been known to the authorities, as she was identified as 'belonging' to Biddenden, this was never made known to the public by the authorities.

If the supposed victim was not attacked, then the following questions remain:

Whose body that was 'naked and much defaced by vermin' was discovered by the authorities?
Was the denial of the murder simply a case of trying to hide the identity of the family of the victim?

- - - o o o - - -

In the spring of 1868, the first of two infanticides occurred near the centre of the village.

Monday, 30th March 1868

Just to the south of the junction between the Sissinghurst Road (A262) and the Headcorn Road (A274) is Henden Hall which was the residence of one James Thurston. It was in the grounds of this property that two lads were raking the bushes out of a pond known locally as the Mill Pond. They discovered a portion of a bag here which, when opened, was found to contain the remains of a newborn female infant in a state of decomposition.

Tuesday, 31st March 1868

The *Maidstone Journal and Kentish Advertiser* reported that the deputy coroner for West Kent, H.J. Farrar, Esq., held an inquest into the child's death in The Rose Inn, Biddenden. O. Haviland Esq., surgeon, deposed to having made a *post mortem* examination of the body and, from the results of the tests applied, he revealed that in all probability, the child was born alive. But as the body had been in the water so long (ten or eleven days at the least), he could not speak with any degree of certainty. The skull was fractured, but whether it was done before disposing of the baby in the water or it came after coming in contact with something that could have been thrown in the water remained an open question. However, such an injury was sufficient to be the cause of death. After hearing all the evidence, it was decided to give the police more time for their investigations by adjourning the inquest until the 16th of April.

Thursday, 16th April 1868

The inquest was resumed and was again adjourned for a month. The coroner stated that he had received certain information, which, if true, might lead to the discovery of the perpetrator of the offence.

After the reports of the discovery and the second inquest, there was no further mention of the incident. This would imply that no progress had been made in the identification of the victim, nor of its mother, and it was decided to proceed no further in an attempt to protect the identity of the mother.

It is almost certain that the child was illegitimate and that the mother was trying to dispose of the evidence. Bastardy in these times was severely looked down upon by society unless it was at the highest social level when it was considered to be an occupational hazard.

Just to emphasise the scale of the problem, a similar discovery was made in the furze on the common by Hungershall Park, in nearby Tunbridge Wells, just two days after the first body was found in Biddenden.

Incidents of infanticide were not unique to Kent and were causing concern all over the country. In Liverpool, the attention of the government was directed to it, with the view that stringent measures should be taken for its suppression. The Home Secretary authorised the borough coroner to offer rewards for the detection of the guilty parties.

On 30th May 1868, the *East Kent Gazette* dedicated a significant part of its editorial to the problem, and the general apathy and indifference upon the subject, by commenting that:

"One of our coroners, a day or two ago, held three inquests on children supposed to have been murdered. The three inquests were all over in an hour or two; in two cases, verdicts of wilful murder were returned, and in the third, there was an open verdict. But who cares about such matters? Three children more or less in the world, or sent out of it by violent hands, what does it matter? Really this would appear to be the careless way in which such facts are regarded. Unhappily the murder of a child creates little sensation. No sooner is one announced, to create a little passing interest, than another child murder is recorded, and still another. One of our coroners had not long since said that the police think no more of finding a dead child than a dead dog. There is some exaggeration there, no doubt, but not much, perhaps. But what of the children who are not

found? For one child murder discovered, perhaps there is at least one that never will be discovered in this world. Can nothing be done to prevent this cruel national custom, as it may sorrowfully be called as much a national custom as exposing infants on the banks of the Ganges or throwing them beneath the car of Juggernaut? The establishment of foundling hospitals and an alteration of the law of affiliation have been proposed and maintained by sound arguments, over and over again; but still, the "Massacre of the Innocents" goes on, and their blood cries aloud, if not for vengeance, for mercy to the children who are to come. And yet England is shamefully apathetic. They are only infants who are burned, drowned, strangled, or mutilated."

- - - o o o - - -

In the spring of 1892, the second infanticide came to light in Biddenden, although it is quite probable that the demise of this unfortunate mite occurred some considerable time before its discovery.

Wednesday, 20th March 1892

Mr Woodgate, a builder of High Halden, was pulling down The Old Chequers Inn (which was to be rebuilt) when he found, concealed between the floor of a bedroom and the plaster of the ceiling of the room below, the skeleton of a child in a box. Around the skeleton was a garment, the whole being black with dirt. The box also contained a quantity of dust. From the size of its head and other bones, it could be said with much certainty that the remains were apparently those of an infant, probably not more than a week old at the time of its death. Lying beside the box was found a bottle of poison, which bore the name of Argles and Stonham, a firm of chemists based in Bank Street, Maidstone.

At the time, the find of the body of the infant found created a considerable sensation in the neighbourhood, but after the initial report in the provincial press, there was no further mention of the discovery, or the cause, even though there was a report of an accident on the same building site in the following July.

As with the 1868 case, it is almost certain that the child was illegitimate and that the mother was trying to dispose of the evidence. The instances of murder of this kind did not seem to be dissipating, as was confirmed by the discovery of another infant which had come to its end in suspicious circumstances in a railway carriage at nearby Ashford just a few weeks afterwards.

- - - o o o - - -

Sources

The Gentleman's Magazine, Volume XLIII, p. 408-409, August 14 1773.

Pile, C.C.R., *Watermills and Windmills of Cranbrook*, Cranbrook & District Local History Society.

Kelly's Directory of Kent, 1882.

The British Library

- *The Burney Collection*
- 18680404 - *Kentish Express Ashford News*
- 18680406 - *Maidstone & Kentish Journal*
- 18680420 - *Maidstone & Kentish Journal*
- 18920423 - *Kentish Gazette and Canterbury Press*
- 18920507 - *Kent Messenger & Maidstone Telegraph*

The British Newspaper Archive

- 17730818 - *Kentish Gazette*
- 17730821 - *Kentish Gazette*
- 17730825 - *Kentish Gazette*
- 17730828 - *Kentish Gazette*
- 17730908 - *Kentish Gazette*
- 18680406 - *Maidstone Journal and Kentish Advertiser*
- 18680411 - *Maidstone Telegraph*
- 18680418 - *East Kent Gazette*
- 18680420 - *Maidstone Journal and Kentish Advertiser*
- 18680530 - *East Kent Gazette*

- 18920422 - *Manchester Evening News*

- 18920423 - *St. James Gazette*

- 18920423 - *Sussex Agricultural Express*

- 18920430 - *Canterbury Journal Kentish Times and Farmers Gazette*

- 18920712 - *Maidstone Journal and Kentish Advertiser*

Kent Messenger Archive

- 18920430 - *South Eastern Gazette*

- 18920712 - *South Eastern Gazette*

Websites

- *www.british-history.ac.uk/survey-kent/vol7/pp478-484*

- *www.maps.nls.uk/* O.S. Map of Kent LXXI, 1876.

Chapter 2 - 1899: Peterson

A murder occurred in Biddenden that attracted great attention, not only nationally but internationally too. What was particularly shocking to the public was that the culprit was the daughter of the parish rector.

Bertha D'Spaen Haggerston Peterson (b. 6th November 1853, d. July 1921)

Bertha Peterson's birth was recorded at Cranbrook, Kent. Her father was the rector at Sissinghurst, Kent and was named William Peterson. Her mother was Harriet Sophia Peterson.

In 1882 William Peterson was offered the rectorship of Biddenden, and as a result, he and his family moved to the rectory adjacent to the parish church of All Saints'. As Bertha was the only surviving daughter, she occupied a special place in the family. She would decorate the church at harvest and Christmas and assist in her father's vestry duties. Being a keen amateur musician, she often performed at village concerts. She was also active at the village school, taking a particular interest in the well-being of the children.

John Whibley (b. February 1861, d. 5ᵗʰ February 1899)

John Whibley's christening was recorded at Biddenden on 17ᵗʰ February 1861. His father was a bootmaker named David Whibley, and his mother was Susanna Whibley. He was a well-known and highly respected tradesman who, like his father, was a bootmaker. Since 1884 he had acted as a correspondent for the *Kent & Sussex Courier* amongst other local publications and was also an Agent of the County Life Assurance Company. He was a much-respected teacher in the Sunday school and was married to Sarah. They had no children.

The events that led up to this crime, which shocked and saddened the world, and those that resulted from it, were as follows:

1883

Alice Gould, aged 11, first met Bertha Peterson, aged 29, at her aunt's school in Nottingham.

Sunday (Easter Day), 17ᵗʰ April 1892

17.30: Bertha's mother, Harriet Peterson, died at Biddenden after she had an epileptic fit and fell into an open fire grate head first. She suffered such serious burns that the facial features of her corpse were unrecognisable. The death had a detrimental effect on Bertha's mental state, and she was observed doing the most unusual things, such as wandering around the streets of Biddenden in broad daylight dressed in just her dressing-gown. She also considered her mother's tragic death to be God's judgement on a sinful village. Her mother's remains were laid to rest four days later in the churchyard of Biddenden's Parish Church.

February 1893

Miss Peterson wrote to Mr Whibley asking him to retire from the Sunday school teachership that they both held in connection with the parish church. She said that if he would not retire, then she would. He refused to acquiesce to her demands, and so she subsequently retired from this position and then wrote to him stating that she felt that she herself should have remained as a teacher. Whibley accused Peterson of being instrumental in preventing his being made superintendent of the Sunday school.

November 1894

The Rev. Walter Raven moved into Biddenden rectory as parish curate.

May 1895

Miss Peterson wrote to Miss Gould saying that a voice had reached her (Miss Peterson), and she knew she (Miss Gould) would be alright in the country. Miss Gould moved into the rectory at Biddenden to live with Miss Peterson. The two women were inseparable, and several contemporaries observed a notable change in Bertha after Alice's arrival. Together the pair began to force their influence on many aspects of village life.

It soon became apparent that both Bertha and Alice had come to hate the Rev. Raven, probably because of his popularity in the parish and the fact that he was taking over more and more of the rector's duties than they thought was desirable. Having fallen ill under the strain of their relationship, Raven moved out of the rectory, leaving the two women and the ageing rector to their own devices.

October 1895

Miss Peterson wrote to the wife of the then Archbishop of Canterbury, Edward White Benson, reporting that a thirty-year-old man in Biddenden had fathered two children with his eighteen-year-old sister. From Bertha and Alice's point of view, heinous crimes such as this could simply be resolved by better educating the men of the parish. Their proposal to create a branch of the White Cross League, an organisation preaching purity and abstinence, in Biddenden never materialised.

Friday, 12th February 1897

Miss Peterson and Miss Gould took away Hester, the daughter of Mrs Gilbert, a widow of Biddenden, to become a servant in the rectory. The girl, aged twelve, had apparently been truanting from school.

14.30: Mrs Gilbert went to the rectory and demanded her child back. Miss Gould came down the stairs in her nightdress and caught Mrs Gilbert by the throat, and pushed her out of the rectory. Mrs Gilbert cried: "Murder!" and a policeman, who was at the door, ordered her off home. Mrs Gilbert and her family never saw Hester again.

Saturday, 6th March 1897

Mary Vane, aged about twelve years and an attendee at the Biddenden Sunday school, was allegedly indecently assaulted by John Whibley. Miss Peterson called upon the child's parents to discuss the matter. Several people stated that Whibley had paid £5 to the child's parents to have the scandal hushed up, and an agreement was signed to that effect.

Tuesday, 16th March 1897

John Whibley received the following letter:

Biddenden Rectory, 16th March 1897.

Mr Whibley.

I have learnt that you are generally thought to have committed an atrocious crime against God and against an innocent, defenceless member of Christ - a little girl. I will not tell you how I learnt this. It is not necessary to do so, seeing that everyone to whom I have applied to clear you is not only unable to give any such evidence but refers me to several more people who are also unable to help my researches in your defence. You are a communicant and a Sunday school teacher, and I ask you, in God's name, two questions:

1. Are you innocent of this crime?

2. Can you tell me how I can clear you?

I will spare neither time, thought, nor money, and no exertion shall be too great for me if you will tell me how to do it. I await your answer.

Bertha S.H. Peterson.

Friday, 26th March 1897

Bertha and Alice held a court of inquiry in which they submitted Whibley to a series of very personal questions. The court was a room in the rectory, and Miss Peterson and Miss Gould took it in turns to act as judge and jury. Miss Gould took notes of the questions and answers. No one else was present except a servant named Alice Cooper, who attended and gave evidence. Whibley swore a solemn oath as to his innocence, but Bertha and Alice were not satisfied with this, and Bertha persuaded her father to chastise Whibley further.

The Rev. William Peterson wrote to John Whibley informing him that he must stay away from Holy Communion and also that he was to cease teaching in the Sunday school until such time as he could clear himself of the crime with which he was charged by Miss Peterson. As a result of this letter Whibley resigned from his Sunday school post.

Miss Peterson wrote seven identical letters outlining the accusation against Whibley and sent them to the Archbishop of Canterbury, the rural dean, the rector (her father), Curate Raven, the two churchwardens, Messrs. Lavance and Pinyon, and the village squire, William Tylden Pattenson. All these letters had reference to the charges of which she had accused Whibley. Mr Lavance received his letter but did not take any action in the matter. The village squire talked to Mary Vane's mother and was convinced of Whibley's innocence. He advised Whibley to take legal action to put pressure on Miss Peterson to withdraw the accusation or face a libel claim, but she ignored it.

During this time, the sapphic couple continued their eccentric lifestyle. At night, Bertha wandered the village streets dressed only in her nightdress, and she let it be known that she shared a bed with Alice and did not care who knew it.

April 1897

William Peterson suffered a seizure during a church service and was totally incapacitated. Bertha knew that her father would soon have to resign as rector. The family was in financial difficulties, so Bertha decided to move into a smaller and cheaper property after they had received the annual tythe payments, which were due in October. Her father could then die in peace, and the life insurance company would have to pay up.

The Misses Peterson and Gould arranged to sell some of the furniture and effects, leaving just enough for the pair of them, the Rev. Peterson, and the child that Bertha had adopted, Hester Gilbert.

The Archbishop of Canterbury, William Temple, was informed of the proposed sale by some well-intentioned villagers, and he ordered Raven to take over the parish duties from Rector Peterson and for Bertha Peterson to pay Raven a stipend out of the rector's income.

Friday, 23rd April 1897

The sale of the rectory property went ahead and raised enough to cover the curate's stipend until 1st October, but Miss Peterson was unhappy about releasing the funds to the curate whom she so hated.

Saturday, 22nd May 1897

Bertha wrote a letter, in her father's name, authorising Raven to be licenced to take sole charge of the parish on the distinct understanding that the archbishop preferred him to another.

Wednesday, 18th August 1897

Mrs Tyler told her next-door neighbour, Mrs Gilbert, that she could see the wicked people taking away her child, Hester, in a cart. Mrs Gilbert replied that Miss Peterson would never let her know any more about her.

Sunday, 26th September 1897

The treatment of the Reverend William Peterson by the two women left a lot to be desired. There were rumours that the old man's room was unheated, his bedclothes unwashed, and his only food was the occasional cup of tea and a piece of cold sausage. The rumours were not too far from the truth and Bertha's two brothers, Edward and William, got to hear of this as well. Whilst Miss Peterson attended the Harvest

Festival service at the church, her brothers and Dr John Harris put the old rector into a carriage and conveyed him to The Bull Hotel at Cranbrook. Here the party spent the night before travelling to William's home in Holsworthy, Devon. In order to avoid being followed, the tyres on both Bertha's and Alice's bicycles were rendered unusable. On returning from church and finding her father missing, Miss Peterson became irate.

John Whibley, encouraged by some of the villagers, exposed the circumstances of the rector's enforced removal in the district and county publications for which he was correspondent. For months afterwards, Miss Peterson continued to persecute Whibley on account of this action.

November 1897
Miss Peterson and Miss Gould left the rectory and went to live in Egerton, a small village near Charing, Kent.

January 1898
Miss Adelaide Oliver, of Kempshall, near Canterbury, who had been on good terms with Miss Peterson during her twelve years residence in Biddenden, received a letter from Miss Peterson expressing her desire to revisit Biddenden and to see old friends. She added that when one was short of money, it made one bad friends with people. She again wrote

shortly after, saying that her position was looking up and expressed another desire to revisit Biddenden and make up with those with whom she had had some misunderstandings and to subscribe to various different charities in the parish.

May 1898

Miss Peterson and Miss Gould applied for several situations between them. Eventually, Miss Peterson was appointed cottage matron at Lady Henry Somerset's Home for Inebriate Women at Duxhurst, Reigate, Surrey. Mrs Emily Cammell, the lady superintendent at Duxhurst, noted Miss Peterson was, from the very first, extremely reserved, very cautious in her movements, odd in her manner and somewhat eccentric.

Tuesday, 23rd August 1898

Whilst at Duxhurst, Miss Peterson wrote to Adelaide Oliver, saying that she was not really a man-hater and that the difficulty was to meet with one who could really be called a man. Sometimes she felt that the fate of Sodom and Gomorrah was hanging over her because of these crimes which were allowed to go unpunished.

October 1898

Mrs Cammell was accused by Miss Peterson of having made private inquiries into her past history. She replied that she had not ever thought of such a thing, let alone carry it into effect. Miss Peterson then said that she would tell Mrs Cammell all about the criminal assault upon a child, of which she felt very much because she could not get anyone to help her to take the matter up. Mrs Cammell asked whether the child had any parents, and Miss Peterson replied that she thought she had a mother but that the woman was to blame for taking 'hushed' money.

Early November 1898

Miss Peterson had a conversation with Sister Eleanor, matron at Duxhurst, in which she was in a very restless, hysterical and excitable condition over the case of Whibley. She told the matron of the rumoured accusations. Sister Eleanor was undoubtedly struck at that time by the curious way in which the case had seemed to take possession of Miss Peterson's mind; so much so that she wrote to Mrs Gould (mother of Miss Peterson's friend) pointing out that Miss Peterson was giving her great anxiety, and that she scarcely liked to leave her alone with the patients. She talked in the wildest way and said she heard a voice telling her to shoot a man in her father's parish. She concluded her letter by asking Mrs Gould to communicate with Miss Peterson's friends.

Mrs Cammell gave Miss Peterson notice to leave her employment, but the notice was later withdrawn.

It was around this time that Miss Gould received a letter from Miss Peterson saying that Sister Eleanor had found out about Mary Vane:

I do not know how she knows or how she got to know, but she asked Mr Hall, the Chaplain at Duxhurst, to say something about it on Sunday, and he came out to talk to me. He looked very straight at me to see if I knew what had been referred to. It was something like this: 'We must have on the whole armour of God, or an evil angel may come and drive us to a great crime. Some men think men who commit great crimes are not men but devils. I (Mr Hall) didn't say we should go so far as that, but we ought ever to wrestle against princes of the power of darkness.' Suppose J.W. is our devil? Our Lord said Judas was, did he not, my lamb?
Your loving Mammie.

December 1898

Miss Peterson again wrote to Miss Gould, saying that Miss Gould needed a mother's love, rest, and quietness and that she had never realised that so much until during the last ten days.

Mrs Cammell gave Miss Peterson written notice to leave her employment at Duxford in January. Miss Peterson requested that the notice be extended to 1st February, which it was.

January 1899

Miss Peterson wrote to Miss Gould, saying that she had been much comforted about her and that she had a distinct message as to her being taken care of. Miss Gould assumed that she meant by that some message from God. She also wrote to many other friends expressing a strong desire to return to Biddenden and be reconciled to all with whom she had quarrelled, including John Whibley. Mrs Cammell wrote to Miss Gould explaining how the notice seemed to have affected Bertha very much and that she had doubts as to her mental balance. She also said that Miss Peterson had told her that she had heard voices telling her to shoot a man in her father's parish. Mrs Cammell said that she was becoming so fearful of Miss Peterson that she was asking Miss Gould to put her into communication with her relatives.

Thursday, 19th January 1899

Alfred Harmer, an assistant at the Army and Navy Stores in London, sold Bertha Peterson a six-chambered, electroplated Colt new patent revolver for £2 7s. 6d. In addition, she purchased a hundred cartridges for the same. Later she took the train from Charing Cross to Pluckley, from where she was driven to Egerton in a cab. On her arrival at the village, she went to the house of a neighbour named Mrs Bartlett, who was in possession of the key belonging to Hillside, where Miss Peterson was to stay in Egerton.

Elizabeth Hope of Hillside Cottage, which adjoined Miss Peterson's residence, was asked by Miss Peterson whether she would be alarmed if she heard the report of a revolver as Miss Peterson was afraid of burglars. She replied in the affirmative. Elizabeth Hope later heard three shots fired at the back of the house. Miss Peterson told Elizabeth Hope that she was as bad as Miss Gould, who had once refused to get into bed with her until she removed a knife which Miss Peterson had placed between the sheets to frighten Miss Gould.

Friday, 20th January 1899

Bertha Peterson visited the grocer's stores of Mr Walter Record in Egerton and procured a piece of sugar box. Repairing to a thicket on the farm of Mr Missing, she placed the piece of wood on a small bush and made it a target for two hours. After her departure, James Wood found the ground covered with empty cartridges and the piece of wood riddled with what was later counted to be forty-two bullet holes.

Tuesday, 24th January 1899

Frank Weller, a librarian of Reigate, received an order for a picture from Bertha Peterson. It was to be a photograph of a picture representing the Good Shepherd, which was well known as a portrayal of "Christ and the lamb," and the suggestion was that Christ was protecting the innocent. Miss Peterson collected the picture the following Saturday.

Wednesday, 1ˢᵗ February 1899

Mr Henry Stapley and Mrs Harriet Stapley, Landlord and landlady of The Rose Inn, Biddenden, received a telegram from Miss Peterson at Duxhurst, saying that she was coming down that day and that they were to have a bedroom in readiness for her.

Miss Peterson arrived at The Rose Inn by bicycle. It was unlikely that she pedalled all the way from Duxhurst, almost fifty miles distant, particularly in the middle of winter and upon wet and muddy rural roads. It was more likely that she and her machine accompanied her luggage, but not the picture, on the train to Headcorn and that she then cycled the four miles to Biddenden from the station. Those standing around the door of the inn when Miss Peterson arrived remarked that they had seldom seen her so vivacious and cheerful. Mrs Stapley was also struck by this pleasantness in her demeanour.

Upstairs with Mrs Stapley, the rector's daughter talked volubly of where she had been and what she had been doing in the interval since last they met. She expressed her intention of staying in Biddenden till the Monday morning, the principal object of her short visit being to present the infant school with the picture. The picture was expected to arrive the following day by bus from Reigate via Headcorn. Her luggage arrived from Headcorn Station later that day and was brought to her by a carrier. She had brought with her the nurse's garb and other belongings, making it clear that she did not intend to return to Duxhurst.

A Biddenden lady asked Miss Peterson the location of Hester Gilbert, and Miss Peterson replied that Hester was in a home.

Thursday, 2nd February 1899

Miss Peterson showed great uneasiness when the day passed without the picture being delivered.

Friday, 3rd February 1899

Bertha Peterson prepared letters, and envelopes addressed to John Whibley, Curate Raven, the two churchwardens and Miss Thirkell. She put these letters into a fancy plaited basket lent to her by Mrs Stapley. Miss Peterson then went to Miss Thirkell's house and told her that she was going to give a kind of peace offering and wanted to make friends with everyone. She suggested that Miss Thirkell might go to the infant school after the morning service on the following Sunday, where her picture was going to be put up. Miss

Thirkell was of the opinion that the agitation in the parish against Mr Whibley had been created and maintained by Miss Peterson even though Miss Thirkell had claimed to be a great friend of Miss Peterson.

17.30: Whilst cycling near Biddenden, Miss Peterson met one of the churchwardens, Mr Lavance, in the roadway and said that she had intended to go to his house to see him and that she was glad to have met him this way. She hoped he did not think it too bad of her to keep Mr Whibley from communion for what she had said about him. Mr Lavance, too was invited to the schoolroom on the following day and accepted with pleasure, shook hands with her, and expressed gladness that bygones should forever be bygones. He noticed nothing in her demeanour at the time to cause any surprise.

That evening Miss Peterson conducted the choir practice, and those who were present later recalled that she only led them with the hymns necessary for the morning service.

Saturday, 4th February 1899

Miss Peterson cycled to Headcorn and made more anxious enquiries about the picture which she was expecting to be delivered from Reigate. This, in due course, arrived in Biddenden. That evening she took the picture down to the village to be fitted with hanging rings. She also paid her lodging bill in advance of her proposed departure on the following Monday.

Mrs Stapley's youngest daughter was charged with delivering the letters to the five recipients. That night, John Whibley received his letter, which read:

Rose Inn, February 4th 1899.

Dear Mr Whibley,

I have had very much in my mind what took place between you and I in the Spring of 1897. Are you willing to forget it? And, if so, what amends do you think you should ask of me? I was wrong in the attitude I took. I believe you were very hardly treated; in any case, it was not for me to judge. Will you come into the Infants' Schoolroom after church tomorrow morning and look at the picture I am giving to the schools and shake hands? I have asked Mr Raven. Mr Pinyon, Mr Lavance, and Miss Thirkell to come, and they will see that I retract what I said about you. I want to give £1 1s to the Foresters or to something that you are interested in, and if you will take it and pass it on to the treasurer, I shall understand that you are willing to forgive and forget.

Yours truly,

B.S.H. Peterson.

Sunday, 5th February 1899

09.00: Mrs Stapley opened Miss Peterson's door to find her on her knees in front of the bed, apparently in prayer. She did not raise her head, and Mrs Stapley withdrew. On the bed lay a copy of the Bible, the Prayer book and *The Golden Butterfly*, a novel about the poor of the East End of London. The bedclothes were all twisted and disarranged in a curious fashion, the pillows being scattered about, plainly indicating that the occupant of the bed had passed an exceedingly restless night. There were also a number of nurses' caps and aprons lying about and several unsealed envelopes containing money lying beside a cashbox.

Bertha Peterson ate her breakfast with relish, not by herself, as usual, but with the family. Afterwards, Harriet Stapley helped Miss Peterson to wrap up the picture of the Good Shepherd in a shawl that Mrs Stapley lent her to protect it from the morning rain. Mrs Stapley saw Miss Peterson leave for the church. Miss Peterson was assisted by Mrs Stapley to pin up her skirts and, with an unusually cheery 'Good morning', walked to the church, passing, on the way, the front door of John Whibley's house. Bertha Peterson later asked the Rev. Raven to meet her in the infants' schoolroom after the morning service.

The inclement conditions caused the local roads and lanes to become muddy and unpleasant, so much so that Mr Lavance, Mr Pinyon and Miss Thirkell all decided to stay at home that morning rather than attend Divine service at the church, and the subsequent meeting with Miss Peterson.

At All Saints' Church, Biddenden, the Rev. Raven conducted the Sunday morning service, and Miss Peterson presided at the harmonium as the regular organist was ill. There were several children sitting near her during the service, and they noticed that she was very restless and constantly putting her right hand to her pocket. Both she and Whibley partook of the Sacrament together.

11.50: John Whibley's residence was just a stone's throw from the school, and on calling in after the service, he informed his wife that he should be away only for a few minutes. Whibley then made his way to the schoolroom porch. Miss Peterson proceeded across the road and met the Rev. Raven. All three entered the infants' schoolroom. Miss Peterson and the Rev. Raven walked to the table in the centre of the room, followed by Mr Whibley. Miss Peterson opened the basket and took out some letters, and said to them both that she wished they would look at the picture. All three walked the six paces to the right to where the picture rested on the harmonium and against the wall. They all then returned to the table in the centre of the room.

Miss Peterson gave one of the envelopes to Mr Whibley, saying: "Ah! Mr Whibley, I wish to present a subscription to the Foresters' Society." She then picked up another envelope, addressed to Mr Lavance, and pushed it towards the Rev. Raven, saying: "Will you see if that is right?" Next, she said to Mr Whibley: "I want you to look well at the picture." Mr Whibley again went towards the picture while the Rev. Raven remained behind the table facing the door. At this point, Bertha Peterson took a revolver from her right-hand pocket, pointed the barrel behind John Whibley's ear, and fired a single shot, killing him instantly. He fell dead at her feet.

The Rev. Raven was looking at the subscription contained in the envelope when he heard the report and, looking round, saw the deceased on the floor with his head towards the picture, with his arms lying flat. At the same time, he dropped the envelope, not having determined its contents. The Rev. Raven saw that Miss Peterson was close to the corpse as she stood with her right hand towards him, facing the curate. Horrified at the suddenness and awful character of the tragedy he had witnessed, the Rev. Raven rushed out for assistance and went to the schoolhouse, where he explained to Mr Arthur Houghton, the schoolmaster, what had occurred.

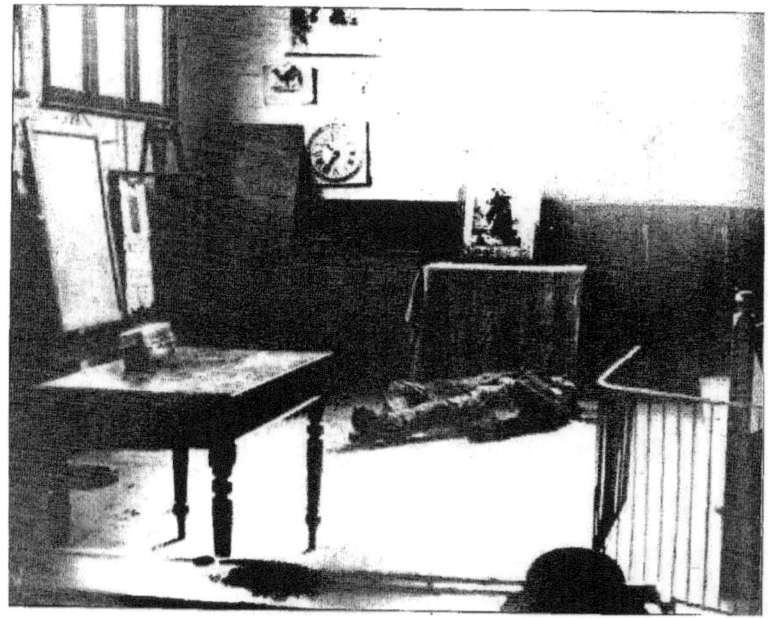

The schoolmaster and his wife, accompanied by the Rev. Raven, arrived at the schoolroom as Miss Peterson appeared at the top of the steps coming out of the schoolroom. She still had the revolver in her right hand. Miss Peterson and the schoolmaster's wife, who had always been on the friendliest of terms, looked at each other. Mrs Houghton broke into tears and cried: "Oh! Miss Peterson. May God forgive you." Miss Peterson replied with evident sincerity: "How sweet of you!" and kissed Mrs Houghton. "You are afraid," she said, adding: "Come with me, and I will let you see him lying there."

Miss Peterson offered Mr Houghton the weapon, of which he gladly relieved her. The Rev. Raven then left to find a doctor. She then came down the steps, and Mr Houghton said: "Oh, Miss Peterson, what made you do this?" She replied: "I had to do it to protect little children." Looking at the gun in Houghton's hand, she said: "You don't seem to understand it. Will you let me have it back, and I will show you how to unload it? There are still five more chambers loaded." Houghton retained his tight grip on the weapon.

Miss Peterson then started taking her leave by moving further along the path and said that she was going to The Rose Inn. Mr Houghton then called to Mr Avery, a harness-maker, who was standing at the back of his premises, which adjoined the schoolyard. Mr Avery went to Mr Houghton and asked him if anything was wrong. He was then told that Miss Peterson had shot someone in the schoolroom. By this time, Miss Peterson was thirty or forty yards away, walking towards the village. Mr Avery rushed after her and caught up with her. He told her that she must come back, but he was told that she did not want to. Mr Avery again told her that she would have to come back and led her towards the school. Miss Peterson said: "I suppose, Mr Avery, you know what I have done this for. I did it in self-defence. I suppose you know a woman is justified in killing a man, as a child is not able. I did that to protect little children." Mr Houghton told a boy to go fetch a policeman, all the while keeping the revolver in his possession. Mr Avery secured Miss Peterson until the police arrived.

The Rev. Raven returned to the schoolroom with Dr Egle Bate, who went into the room where he saw the body of a man lying on his back. His left arm was on his breast with the right leg drawn up, and there was a large pool of blood under him. The doctor also noticed a letter was lying on the harmonium, just above the head of the deceased, addressed to Mr Whibley. It contained two half-sovereigns and a shilling, with a memorandum that it was a subscription for the Foresters. There were other letters on the table.

P.C. Mungeham arrived at the schoolroom, where Mr Houghton handed him the revolver. The constable joined the doctor in the schoolroom, where he too saw the body of Whibley lying on the ground with blood running from his right ear. Dr Bate confirmed that Whibley was dead. Coming out of the school, the P.C. saw Miss Peterson detained by Mr Avery, who was holding her by the wrists. He told her that he would charge her with killing Whibley, and she replied: "Very well." The constable then took Miss Peterson over the road to The Chequers Inn, where the landlord allowed them to use his private quarters. Here she asked the constable if he was married, to which he answered that he was. He then cautioned her. She added: "You have no children, I suppose? I had to do this. Where have you gentlemen been to allow this man to outrage little children?" He then took her to Cranbrook Police Station, some five miles distant, and handed her over to Superintendent Thomas Fowle.

13.15: The superintendent took Miss Peterson into custody and informed her that she would be charged with feloniously and with malice aforethought, killing John Whibley by shooting him with a revolver at Biddenden. Fowle cautioned Peterson in the usual way, and she again confessed that she had indeed shot him. She was detained in the cells and said: "I only have to say that there is no malice and that I should not call it murder."

Superintendent Fowle returned to the school, where he saw Whibley's lifeless body. He examined the cadaver and found a wound at the back of the head, a pool of blood under the head, and also a pool under the right ear. He surmised that death had been instantaneous and that life had long been extinct. On the desk of the schoolroom, he saw a black shawl, and on the desk nearest the table, a hat and walking stick belonging to the deceased. On the table, he found some envelopes. One was addressed to Mr John Whibley and contained £1 1s, with a memorandum inside stating: "Subscription to day school. February 4th 1899," and signed B.S.H. Peterson. He also noticed other envelopes addressed to Miss Thirkell, G.B. Pinyon Esq. and Mr Henry Lavance, with some pieces of paper. There was a half-sovereign in one. There was also a piece of paper marked: "For the Zenana Mission."

The superintendent then proceeded to The Rose Inn and examined Miss Peterson's property. He found among it a box containing forty-three cartridges. Mrs Stapley handed two parcels of clothing, a cash box containing numerous articles and a hatbox to the police officer, which he removed as evidence. At Cranbrook Police Station, Fowle made a detailed examination of the chattels taken from The Rose Inn. In the cashbox, he found two boxes, one of which contained the cartridges and a rod for cleaning the barrel of the revolver. He also found the receipt for the framing of the photograph of the Good Shepherd for £1 5s. There was a paper bearing a picture of the weapon, showing it open and closed, which was with the cartridges. Also, he found a copy of *The Maiden Tribute of Modern Babylon*, a pamphlet written by Mr W.T. Stead, an extremely strong article on modern immorality in London and a copy of the Criminal Law Amendment Act. There was also a quantity of other correspondence.

Monday, 6th February 1899
The press descended upon Biddenden and Cranbrook, and the story instantly became a national sensation.

Miss Peterson was brought up at Cranbrook Police Court before the presiding magistrate, Mr J.B. Jobson. Since her arrest, she had been detained in the cells at Cranbrook. She was dressed in a fawn-coloured tailor-made coat and skirt, with a heavy fur cape thrown around her shoulders. Her face wore a rather concerned look, but she gave no sign of agitation. She took her stand in front of the magistrate's table between two policemen and gave her full name as Bertha Haggerston Peterson, and was described as a spinster. The charge against her was read out: "On 5th of February, she feloniously, wilfully, and of her malice aforethought did kill and murder one John Whibley." She listened to the charge as it was read over but said nothing. She seemed wholly unconcerned and betrayed, and showed no emotion whatever.

Superintendent Fowle then gave evidence as to his actions of the previous day and asked the magistrate to remand the prisoner for a reasonable time. The magistrate acceded to the policeman's request by announcing: "Bertha Haggerston Peterson, you are remanded until 14th February, at the Vestry Hall, Cranbrook." Miss Peterson responded in an unconcerned way, "Thank you," and after a pause, "Is that all?" Superintendent Fowle responded, "Yes, that is all at present, Miss Peterson." The prisoner then walked back to her cell, followed by two constables.

Biddenden School was closed for the whole day as it was to be used for the inquest that was to be held in the main classroom. However, in the school logbook, Mr Houghton made no attempt to glorify the events of the previous day but simply recorded, "The school was closed today because of a terrible accident which befell one of the villagers."

"That evening the coroner's inquiry into the circumstances attending the death of John Whibley was held in the schoolroom at Biddenden. Miss Peterson declined to attend, and though her family was represented by Mr. H.C. Gollen, instructed by Mr. George Hamilton, this gentleman did not appear on her behalf. The inquest was presided over by Mr C. Duncan Murton, coroner for the Cranbrook Division of Kent. Unusually, for an English inquest, the medical men, after their post mortem examination, replaced the deceased in the position in which he fell. In the end, furthest from the door, beneath a window, was stretched the murdered man, deprived, however, of coat, waistcoat and boots. There was still a pool of blood under the head, and the features were livid, but the eyes were closed. Just behind the body was the harmonium, covered with baize, and upon it, the picture, in a grey-green mount, framed in reeded walnut.

Evidence of identification was given by Sarah Whibley, the victim's widow, who produced the letter received on Saturday night inviting her husband to the school after Sunday's service. Mrs. Whibley said that it was the suggestion in this letter that her husband was asked to forgive. He was ready to do so, and went to school to meet Miss Peterson as requested, and that Miss Peterson and her husband had not been on good terms.

Coroner: Did you know anything of the dispute between your husband and Miss Peterson?

Mrs Whibley: I think she was jealous of him in the Sunday school. Mr Whibley had said, "If you want my class, Miss Peterson, take it; but I don't want you to interfere in it."

A large quantity of other correspondence was then produced, including the accusative missive of 16th March 1897, to which Mrs Whibley admitted to being conversant but declared, indignantly, that there was no truth in the letter.

Coroner: Did you understand that it was that dispute to which Miss Peterson referred?
Mrs Whibley: I don't think that was the commencement of it.
Coroner: But do you think that that was the charge Miss Peterson referred to in the letter of 4th February 1899?
Mrs Whibley: That was the one. She was bitter against him for a year or two before, and she had written disagreeable letters to other people before that.

Dr Joshua Law Kerr described the results of the *post mortem* examination. He had found a wound commencing at the aperture of the right ear, passing through the base inwards and upwards into the base of the brain. The bullet produced as evidence was found there, and the witness was of the opinion that the injury to the brain caused by it produced death. There was no external mark beyond the bruising of the right ear, which he attributed to the impact of the bullet. Death must have been instantaneous.

The coroner, in addressing the jury, pointed out that the cause of death was a bullet wound in the head. The only other question was how the wound was caused. He considered that the evidence of Mr Raven was conclusive on that point. They would also remember that when Miss Peterson gave the revolver to Mr Houghton, it was loaded in five chambers; and that she made an effort to get away but was detained. There was no doubt that death was caused by a bullet and that the wound was inflicted by a shot from a revolver fired by Miss Peterson. If that was so, they could only come to one conclusion. They could not say that the crime was unpremeditated, having regard to the fact that a definite appointment was made to meet Mr Whibley.

The jury returned a verdict of wilful murder against Bertha Peterson.

Tuesday, 7th February 1899
Miss Peterson was conveyed by an early morning train on the South Eastern Railway from Cranbrook to the County Gaol at Maidstone. She was at once admitted to the infirmary, where she was watched day and night. In the

course of the next few days, she was examined by a specialist in lunacy who had been sent down by the Home Office.

John Whibley's death was not the only tragic incident to occur in the Biddenden area at that time. After going to the railway station which was near his farm, in order to see the departure of Miss Peterson, William Unicume took his gun to go rabbit shooting. While getting through a gap in the hedge, surrounded by brambles, he slipped on the wet soil, causing his gun to go off. The charge struck him on the face, one side of which was blown away. He was found shortly afterwards by his wagoner. Notwithstanding his fearful injuries, Unicume lived for nearly an hour before his demise.

Biddenden School was again closed for the day while a carpenter attempted to plane off the bloodstains from the floor. It was finally decided that the boards should be removed and replaced with new ones so that Miss Bradshaw, the infants' mistress, and the little ones might have as few mementoes of the occurrence as possible.

Bertha Peterson wrote to Miss Gould at Bradbourne College, Sevenoaks, saying: "God commanded me to do this for Him. It is alright, I weep for you. I am perfectly content. God prompts me not to be frightened." Apparently, Miss Peterson's only regret at this time was that Miss Gould would be unhappy. She also wrote to Sister Eleanor at Duxhurst, saying: "I have got myself into trouble by shooting a man. I beg you to see what you can do for my little girl at Bradbourne College, Sevenoaks. I do not know how she can bear the consequences. If anyone can comfort her, you can. Will you go to her?"

Wednesday, 8th February 1899
Biddenden School re-opened to its teachers and pupils.

During her time in gaol, Miss Peterson wrote many letters, a number of these being sent to Alice Gould. She wrote:

"God told me to do what I have done. I shot this man 'J.W.' If you knew how I felt, dear, it would help you to bear up. I am quite happy, except for you. This will break your heart, but God has told me to do it. I have no fear; I am content, my own lamb. If our hearts are broken, and if we have to go through agony, we shall have been partly the means of saving little girls. God has told me that you will be consoled, and that he will make you happy" and;

"God has told me that you will have another mother. S.E. will be your mother. There is no one in the world like her. I love you, my lamb. I am very comfortable here, and can do almost what I like" and;

"My own darling little one. - Come to me, for I am detained here for something I have done. I should quite happy if it were not for you. Sister Eleanor will console you. I love you always, ma belle, ma petite. - Your loving Bertha" and; *"I suppose J.W. is a devil. Our Lord said Judas was one."*

She also wrote again to Sister Eleanor, saying: "I want my little girl kept away from people who will tell her too much, and from seeing the newspapers, and above all from coming here by herself."

Friday, 10th February 1899

From the funeral of John Whibley, the *London Evening Standard* reported that:

"The blinds of almost every house in the village were drawn, whilst, in addition to the numerous relations and friends, a number of the parishioners and nearly a hundred members of the Foresters' Courts in the district attended. The coffin and bier were covered with wreaths. The service both in the church and at the graveside was conducted by the Rev. W.M. Clarke, of St. Michael's, the Rev. W. Raven, curate-in-charge of Biddenden, being too unwell to attend."

Wednesday, 15th February 1899

Bertha Peterson was brought again before Mr Jobson at Cranbrook, charged with the murder of John Whibley and was formally remanded until the following Tuesday. The prisoner entered the court in a faltering manner, using both her hands to assist her down the two steps. Superintendent Fowle asked for a remand, stating that the Treasury had been communicated with, and he hoped to complete the case by the day mentioned. The prisoner, when informed by the Magistrate that she was remanded, simply responded: "Yes." Crowds of people assembled outside the Courthouse, and some inside the building attempted to confront her as she was bustled back to her cell by the constables.

Friday, 17th February 1899

A further tragedy occurred when a farmer named Witherden, who had resided in the parish of Biddenden all his life, was engaged in a conversation respecting the murder when he became overcome with excitement and, after saying: "I shall die," expired. Death was due to syncope brought on by excitement.

Tuesday, 21st February 1899

Miss Peterson, having been conveyed from the County Gaol at Maidstone to Cranbrook on the previous evening, was charged at the Police-court in the Vestry Hall with the wilful murder of John Whibley. Mr S. Pearce, solicitor to the Treasury Department, prosecuted while Mr C.F. Gill and Mr H.C. Gollan, instructed by Mr George Hamilton, appeared for the defence. The court was crowded to its utmost capacity. The prisoner walked firmly to the dock, seemed totally unconcerned, and frequently turned to smile at someone in the body of the Vestry Hall. However, her careworn look showed the mental suffering she had undergone in gaol. She was dressed in the usual fur cape, black dress, and coloured felt hat trimmed with feathers. She carried a bunch of violets and lilies of the valley sent to her by Miss Gould. A special force of constables was in readiness in case of any attempt upon the prisoner, this being considered likely, in view of the demonstration shown against her the previous week. The Clerk read over the charge, but the prisoner made no answer.

Mr Pearce, in opening for the prosecution, traced the prisoner's history and connection with the deceased and her quarrel with him in 1893 and 1897 and gave details of a correspondence passing between the two, including a letter from Whibley denying the imputations against his character. He also read letters from the prisoner to Miss Gould, written since the crime was committed.

Mrs Whibley gave evidence as to the receipt by her husband of a letter from the prisoner inviting him to come to the infant school after church. She said that Miss Peterson and the deceased had many disagreements, and she thought Miss Peterson was jealous of him in the Sunday school.

Other witnesses repeated their previous statements.

Evidence was then called from Dr Egle Bate, who described the nature of Whibley's injuries, and that he had known the accused for eight years. He would not say she was insane, but she was bordering on it and, at times, seemed extremely odd. She was a woman very susceptible to suggestions, readily liable to the influence of others, and was extremely eccentric and decidedly emotional. He said that Miss Peterson had expressed to him, great interest in the White Cross League. He also said that Mrs Peterson, the prisoner's mother, had been subject to epilepsy and that he was called in when she died after falling on the fire during an epileptic seizure.

Alice Gould deposed that her acquaintance with the accused had extended over the past fifteen years. The witness said that the accused had been, and still is, much attached to her. They had seen one another very often. She had received many letters from Miss Peterson, including some since she had been in gaol. She further said that Miss Peterson was keenly interested in religious matters and also in the question of protecting children. Miss Peterson took an active interest in the Criminal Law Amendment Act movement. She had taken one child from the village and provided for it. She was also deeply concerned with the aims of the White Cross League and was anxious that its work should be encouraged in Biddenden by the parishioners. She confirmed that she had lived at the rectory at Biddenden with the accused and her father for some time, later going with Miss Peterson to Egerton. Subsequently, they both entered the service of a clergyman named Charles Henry Bulmer, of the cider-making family in Herefordshire. They left the service together; there was some unpleasantness, and they did not like the servant-maid work. Later they took lodgings at Clapham Junction. From there, Miss Peterson went to Duxhurst, and the witness remained in London. They corresponded frequently. While the witness lived with Miss Peterson, the latter was very strange in her manner, minimising great things and magnifying small things. Her recent letters were very incoherent and grew more and more so. These letters are numbered in hundreds. In one, she wrote: "We must have on the whole armour of God, including H.C., or any angel may swoop down upon us." The witness took H.C. to mean Holy Communion. Miss Gould said that the prisoner had spoken to her about insanity in her family:

Mr Gill: Was she anxious about eternal punishment?
Miss Gould: That was only when she was quite young.
Mr Gill: Did she speak of people being punished in this world?
Miss Gould: No.
Mr Gill: Do you know that she is now quite contented and happy.
Miss Gould: Yes, she believes that God has forgiven her.
Mr Gill: She is forty-five, and you are only twenty-seven.

Continuing, Miss Gould said that she regarded Miss Peterson as an extremely kind-hearted woman, extremely unselfish and good.

The Rev. Henry Hall, a chaplain to Lady Henry Somerset's Homes at Duxhurst, informed the court that he had come to the conclusion that the prisoner's mind was affected, as she spoke incoherently and in a rambling manner, and that she was not capable of forming a right judgment. She was also fond of repeating: "God has forgiven me my sins."

For the defence, evidence was given showing that several of the prisoner's relations had died in asylums and that she was thought to be a monomaniac, a person who has an obsessive enthusiasm for one thing. Drs. Joyce and Harris gave the opinion that the prisoner was not of a sound mind.

The prisoner was committed for trial at the next Assizes at Maidstone.

Monday, 13th March 1899

The Rev. William Peterson, after deteriorating in health as a result of the murder, died at Holsworthy, North Devon. He was nearly ninety years of age.

Wednesday, 24th March 1899

Frances Davis, medical superintendent of the Kent County Lunatic Asylum at Barming, visited Miss Peterson in Maidstone Gaol and interviewed her to ascertain the state of her mind. He came to the conclusion she was suffering from hallucinations.

Sunday, 26th March 1899

Miss Peterson was taken ill in Maidstone Gaol.

Saturday, 1st April 1899

Miss Peterson had been so ill that she was removed to the prison infirmary and placed on an invalid's diet.

Friday, 7th April 1899

Frances Davis, on the instruction of the Treasury, had interviewed Bertha Peterson whilst in custody. In court, he reeled off a long list of attributes identified during his examinations which indicated Bertha Peterson's sanity, or lack thereof.

Saturday, 15th April 1899

The Illustrated Police News reported that:

"The specialist's report upon the state of mind of Miss Bertha Peterson, who was committed for trial at Maidstone Assizes, had now been presented to the Home Secretary. The report certified Miss Peterson to be of unsound mind and suffering from strange impressions and hallucinations. The officials at Maidstone Gaol were awaiting the decision of the Home Secretary as to whether Miss Peterson should be removed to an asylum. The brothers of Miss Peterson acted in a generous manner towards Mrs. Whibley, and undertook to pay the whole of her legal expenses incurred by the murder. It was decided to erect a monument over Whibley's grave, the cost being defrayed by public subscription."

Similarly, it was reported in *The Illustrated Police Budget*, that:

"As a result of the close watch that has been kept by experts in insanity on Miss Bertha Peterson.... it has been conclusively proved that she suffers from attacks of epilepsy, which at times make her unaccountable for her actions. As her mother was subject to epileptic fits, in one of which she fell on the fire and was burned to death. The defence, which will be put forward at the trial at the assizes in May, will be similar to that pleaded at the trial of Boakes, the Riverhead murderer, who, it will be remembered, shot his sweetheart, Miss Lawrence, in the highway. It was then proved by medical experts that epilepsy made Boakes unaccountable for his actions and was ordered to be detained as a criminal lunatic."

Wednesday, 19th April 1899

Mrs Sophia Baskerville Newman, aunt to Miss Peterson and one of the most important witnesses for the defence, who gave evidence at the Police Court in regard to the mental antecedents, died at Edmonton, Middlesex.

Thursday, 1st June 1899

It was reported in *The Morning Post* that:

"As a result of the medical supervision of Miss Peterson that she had been certified as being in a fit medical condition to

*plead. She was to be put on trial at the Kent Assizes, which
were to open at Maidstone on 10th July."*

Friday, 7th July 1899

Dr Frances Davis visited Miss Peterson in Maidstone Gaol,
where she was calm, collected and without a suspicion of
remorse for what she had done. The prisoner had both
spoken and written to him on the question of insanity. She
objected to being thought insane. Her idea was that if the
direction given to her was a reasonable and good one, it was
not insanity to follow it, but if the direction was foolish or
wicked, it would be insanity to follow it.

Tuesday, 11th July 1899

In opening the Kent Assizes at Maidstone, Mr Justice
Mathew, in his charge to the Grand Jury, briefly referred to
the charge against Miss Peterson of murdering John Whibley
at Biddenden. He said that if the jury were satisfied that the
deceased was killed by the wilful act of the accused, it would
be their duty to return a true bill against her. The question as
to Miss Peterson's insanity would have to be dealt with by
the petty jury. The Grand Jury later in the day returned a true
bill against Miss Peterson. The defence to be set up was that
the accused was insane at the time she committed the deed.

Wednesday, 12th July 1899

The Assizes continued, and Bertha Peterson was indicted for the wilful murder of John Whibley. The court was crowded, with many women being present. The prisoner was dressed in black, evidently intended as a sign of mourning for her late father. She was perfectly calm and composed, and throughout the whole hearing, which lasted several hours, she watched the various witnesses with a great deal of interest and listened attentively to the learned counsel. She was given a seat in the dock and pleaded guilty in a clear, firm voice, but at the request of her counsel, his Lordship consented to enter the plea as one of not guilty.

Mr H.F. Dickens Q.C., with Mr G.J. Talbot, conducted the prosecution on behalf of the Treasury, the prisoner being represented by Mr C.F. Gill Q.C. and Mr A. Gill. In his opening statement, Mr Dickens said he was instructed by the Treasury to lay before the jury the evidence in this case. It was a very painful and distressing one from every point of view, and there could be no question that the deed was committed by the prisoner. The main issue that they would have to determine was the condition of the lady's mind at the time the deed was committed. The murder was either one of the most cold-blooded, barbarous nature, committed by a person apparently utterly callous; or it was one committed by a lady who, by reason of the failure of the action of the brain or disease of that organ, was under such delusions at the time that she committed the crime, that she thought the deed was committed by command of Almighty God, in order to right a wrong which had, or which she thought had been done.

Mr Dickens then described, in detail, all the events leading up to and including the murder and then continued: Having regard to the nature of the offence, to the previous history of the prisoner, to the correspondence, to the cold-blooded callousness of the prisoner, contrasted with the state of mind apparent in her letters in which she expressed a wish to be reconciled to everyone, and remembering that she had had no connection at all with Whibley since 1897. The Treasury, in justice to her, ordered two doctors to watch her very carefully and report upon what they learned from her as to her state of mind. They would not be competent to state whether the prisoner was insane at the time she committed the murder, but they would give such evidence as came within their cognizance. There is no doubt she did what she believed to be right and that which God commanded her to do. She told Dr Davies, for instance, that men were all-powerful. She had tried to get the matter ventilated but had failed, and God had directed her to do the deed, to purchase the revolver and practise with it and then to shoot Whibley, and not only Whibley but as many other men as she could get together at the same time. Certainly, the impression left upon Dr Davies' mind was that the other persons present at the time of the murder had very narrow escapes.

Mr Gill called evidence of the death, since the murder, of the prisoner's aunt, Mrs Newman, who was to have been an important witness for the defence. The aunt's depositions, taken at the magisterial hearing, were to the effect that the prisoner's mother was a member of a family of ten, eight of whom had died from consumption and the other two from brain affections. Various other members of the family also displayed mental weakness.

Dr Charles Hoar, the prison chaplain at Maidstone, said that the prisoner has been under his charge since February. She was quiet and well behaved, happy and perfectly contented. She showed no signs of depression or remorse for what she had done. She read and wrote a great deal. She at first objected to his conversing with her except on strictly medical grounds. She held that it was not his duty to inquire into her state of mind. Subsequently, she had told him that she had had a divine command to shoot Whibley and that she had planned the whole thing out. She said Whibley was all right, presuming that there was no such thing as eternal torment, which she said is a good thing for him and for the cause which she had at heart. She added that she would do the same thing again if she had the opportunity. Her one object was the protection of little children.

At this point, his Lordship addressed the jury, saying that they had heard the opinion of two experts and that if they were satisfied that the prisoner was suffering from delusion and acted under the influence of such delusion and that it was due to disease of the brain, she would be entitled to be acquitted of the charge on the ground that she was not responsible for the crime. They should determine whether they thought the case should go on or whether they would desire to hear counsel for the defence. If only one of their number wished it to go on, it would be sufficient, but if they were all satisfied with the evidence offered, the case need not proceed.

After some conversation, the foreman of the jury said that two of their number wanted the case to go on.

Dr Hoar then continued and said he was satisfied that the prisoner was perfectly sincere in all she had said. She pointed out to him that she did not state the truth when she summoned five persons to meet her in the schoolroom but said she was justified in doing as she did. In carrying out her work, she became adept at deceit. On the previous day, he had a long conversation with her when she said men had no sense of right or wrong. Only a woman could understand those things. It was very difficult to get justice in England, and by making a stir in the world, she hoped it would influence others to alter the laws. She was very glad she had made a stir.

Mr Gill then called evidence to prove that insanity was prominent in members of the prisoner's family on her mother's side and then proceeded to deal with the evidence at great length, pointing out how the case of Whibley had constantly become more and more present in her mind, and how nearly all the witnesses had spoken of the prisoner's eccentricity. Before learned counsel had concluded his address, the foreman of the jury intimated that they had come to a decision.

The jury then formally found that the prisoner was guilty of the murder of John Whibley but that at the time, she was mentally weak and not criminally responsible for her actions.

His Lordship directed that the prisoner should be kept in strict custody until Her Majesty's pleasure was known.

Monday, 17th July 1899

Miss Peterson left Maidstone Gaol for Broadmoor Criminal Lunatic Asylum, Berkshire. She was accompanied by a warder and wardress and appeared to be in very good spirits. She was, however, reluctant to leave the prison, where she said she had been very happy during the whole time of her incarceration, now nearly six months. None of Bertha Peterson's relatives had visited her since her conviction, but she had been seen by three personal friends, to whom it is understood she expressed her dissatisfaction at the result of her trial and further stated that she would rather have been hanged than confined in an asylum for the rest of her life.

July 1921

Bertha D'Spaen Haggerston Peterson died in Broadmoor Criminal Lunatic Asylum, Berkshire, aged sixty-eight years.

Finally, one has to have some sympathy for John Whibley, who, as a result of his own death, missed the greatest scoop that any Biddenden local correspondent could have wished for since the demise of the Chulkhurst conjoined twins.

Sources

Bygone Kent, Volume II, pp. 500-503; The Long Blue Line - The Fowle Family's 165 Years of Police Service.

Joy, Angie (Transcribed by), *Burials in the Parish of Biddenden in the County of Kent - 1877-1992*, July 2009.

Adams, Ed, *The Cranbrook Journal*, No. 25, A Victorian Anglican: William Peterson of Sissinghurst and Biddenden. 2014.

Adams, Ed, *The Cranbrook Journal*, No. 26, The Biddenden Murder, 1899. 2015.

True Detective, pp. 11-14; Death in the Classroom. June 1991.

The British Library

- 18920423 - *Kentish Express and Ashford News*
- 18920426 - *Maidstone and Kentish Journal*

The British Newspaper Archive

- 18920426 - *Maidstone & Kentish Journal*
- 18990206 - *London Evening Standard*
- 18990207 - *Morning Post, London*
- 18990208 - *Kent & Sussex Courier*
- 18990209 - *Maidstone Journal and Kentish Advertiser*
- 18990211 - *Illustrated Police Budget*
- 18990211 - *London Evening Standard*
- 18990212 - *Lloyds Weekly Newspaper*
- 18990215 - *London Evening Standard*
- 18990218 - *Bradford Daily Telegraph*
- 18990221 - *Pall Mall Gazette*

- 18990221 - *Globe*

- 18990224 - *Sevenoaks Chronicle and Kentish Advertiser*

- 18990303 - *Surrey Mirror*

- 18990316 - *London Evening News*

- 18990401 - *Globe*

- 18990414 - *The West Australian*

- 18990415 - *Illustrated Police Budget*

- 18990415 - *Illustrated Police News*

- 18990520 - *The Neihart Herald*

- 18990601 - *Morning Post*

- 18990704 - Surrey *Mirror*

- 18990711 - *Pall Mall Gazette*

- 18990711 - *Globe*

- 18990713 - *London Daily News*

- 18990713 - *London Evening Standard*

- 18990713 - *London Daily News*

- 18990713 - *Maidstone Journal and Kentish Advertiser*

- 18990714 - *Kent & Sussex Courier*

- 18990720 - *Maidstone Journal and Kentish Advertiser*

  ### Websites

- www.findagrave.com/cgibin/fg.cgi?page=gr&GRid=11 9473420.

- www.findmypast.co.uk (England & Wales, Crime, Prisons & Punishment, 1770-1935 and England & Wales, Births, 1837-2006)

- www.sbcofe.org/wpcontent/uploads/2014/05/Burials_alphabetical.pdf.

Chapter 3 – 1971: Pankhurst

A walk through All Saints' churchyard in Biddenden may lead the reader to the final resting place of a mother and her five young children, all, arguably, the victims of the most notorious murderer known to Biddenden.

Richard Thomas Pankhurst (b. 1940)
Richard Pankhurst's birth was recorded at Hollingbourne, Kent, in quarter two of 1940, his mother having the maiden name of Roberts. He was an unemployed builder's labourer.

Margaret Wendy A. Pankhurst (b. 21st May 1942, d. 23rd June 1971).
Wendy Pankhurst's date of birth appeared as 21st May 1942 on the registration of her death. She was married to Richard Pankhurst in October 1961, and they had five children: Susan, aged 9, Nicholas, 6, Sarah, 5, Aubrey, 3, and Garry, 2.

The events that were to lead up to this crime, and those that resulted from it, were as follows:

Tuesday, 22nd June 1971
Evening: Mrs Christine Stephens, sister of Thomas Pankhurst, saw her brother and his family. She knew how

much he liked to play with them and make them sing. Mrs Stephens noticed that her brother seemed more cheerful than of late, having been depressed recently. He told her that he was going into Tenterden the next day for a prescription for some new medication.

A neighbour knocked on the Pankhursts' door and asked to borrow ten pence for the meter from Mrs Pankhurst. She did not have the money and said: "We are broke but happy".

Wednesday, 23rd June 1971
Early morning: In their semi-detached, three-bedroomed council house at 51, Chulkhurst, Biddenden, Thomas Pankhurst murdered his wife and five children. The family's pet dog, Tonto, was heard howling into the night.

04.00: Pankhurst climbed a fourteen-foot-high electricity transformer in a field opposite the end of Chulkhurst at its junction with the A262, the Biddenden to Sissinghurst road. He attempted to commit suicide by grabbing at the electric terminals. The resultant shock and bolt threw him onto the barbed wire apron below. He suffered severe burns and a broken ankle.

04.30: Pankhurst's screams awoke one of the local residents who subsequently knocked on the door of 7, Chulkhurst, almost opposite the electricity transformer. The residents of number 7, Mr and Mrs Farris, were told of the events at the transformer, and Mr Farris dialled 999 to summon the emergency services.

Charles Pankhurst, who lived nearby, also heard his brother's screams and went to the transformer to investigate. He was supporting the injured man caught in the barbed wire when the police arrived.

04:45: Police, led by Detective Superintendent Ted Jenvey, deputy chief of Kent C.I.D., went to the Pankhurst's house and forced open the front door. They were confronted with a gruesome scene. The blood-soaked body of Mrs Pankhurst was found lying on a bed with one of her children. The other four youngsters were lying on their beds in a second bedroom. The throats of all six had been cut.

Thomas Pankhurst was taken to Maidstone's West Kent Hospital and two hours later was transferred to the specialist burns unit at Queen Victoria Hospital, East Grinstead, West Sussex. He was described as being in a very distressed condition. Here he was kept under police guard. A police officer was also put on guard outside their house at Biddenden.

10.00: The bodies were carried from the house on stretchers. Scores of police officers and tracker dogs with handlers searched the nearby roads and fields for the murder weapon. Meanwhile, uniformed officers sealed off the house as senior detectives worked inside.

Being interviewed by members of the press, stunned neighbours said that the Pankhursts kept very much to themselves and that they had only been living there for a few months. One woman, who lived nearby, said that she thought that Mr Pankhurst had been off work for some while, whilst neighbour Mrs Doris Feeny, said that the family had many relatives in the village.

Thursday, 24th June 1971

Police were still waiting to interview the badly injured Pankhurst, who remained critically ill with severe burns at the East Grinstead hospital.

Despite its enormity, the case received very little coverage in the national press. Just a few lines appeared in the *Daily Telegraph*, the *Daily Mail* and *The Sun*. The *London Evening Standard* and *The Guardian* chose to omit all reference to the incident. Perhaps this was a sign of the violent times being then experienced in England. This was made even more evident when, the very next day, the murder of a family of four in Halifax received similar indifferent treatment by the media.

Friday, 25th June 1971

At the Queen Victoria Hospital, East Grinstead, Pankhurst had his left arm amputated because of the severe burning sustained during his activities on the electricity transformer.

Tuesday, 29th June 1971

14.15: Pankhurst travelled by ambulance from the hospital in East Grinstead to Cranbrook Magistrates' Court. Two police officers, a nursing sister and two attendants accompanied him in the vehicle. Extra police were on duty when he arrived. Because of his severe injuries, a special court was convened inside the ambulance, in the court car park, with a police guard around the vehicle. The head of East Kent C.I.D., Superintendent Harold Blackburn, explained that Pankhurst was considered well enough to be moved to another hospital but not well enough to be moved up to the courtroom. He was a big man, weighing seventeen stones.

14.30: The prisoner was also accompanied in the ambulance by his brother, Charles, his sister, Christine, and his solicitor, Mr Thomas Hulme, of Folkestone. Pankhurst was charged by Detective Inspector Frederick Wood, head of Ashford

C.I.D., with: "At Biddenden on a date unknown between June 21st and June 24th he murdered Mrs Margaret Wendy Anne Pankhurst, aged 29, contrary to common law". Mr William Tipples, the magistrate, asked Pankhurst if he wished to say anything. Pankhurst replied: "No". Throughout the hearing, he remained lying, covered in a sheet with only his head showing. Superintendent Michael Foley of Ashford told the court that Mrs Pankhurst's body was one of six found dead in her home at Biddenden, the others being her five children. He asked for a remand in custody until the following Monday. This was granted. The ambulance hearing, which had lasted barely two minutes, was over.

Thomas Pankhurst was then remanded in custody to Brixton Prison Hospital until 5th July and was taken on the two-hour drive there in the back of the ambulance. There was a police escort.

Monday, 5th July 1971

Pankhurst was remanded in custody for a further week by Cranbrook magistrates. He did not attend the hearing as he was still in Brixton Prison Hospital being treated for his injuries.

Monday, 12th July 1971

At Cranbrook court, the case against Pankhurst was further adjourned for a week. Again, Pankhurst was not in attendance. He was remanded in custody for the third time on the simple charge of murdering his wife. Cranbrook magistrates were told that Pankhurst's condition was still too serious to allowing him to attend court.

Tuesday, 13th July 1971

At Cranbrook, the inquest into the death of Wendy Pankhurst and her five children was told by the coroner, Mr J.E. Clarke, that her husband had been charged with their murder. Evidence of identification of the bodies was given by Mrs Pankhurst's brother-in-law, Mr Robert E. Brown. Mr Clarke ordered that the bodies be cremated and that the inquest be adjourned until Tuesday, 16th November. However, it would appear that this order was not obeyed, as Wendy Pankhurst and her five children were later buried together in the churchyard of All Saints' Church, Biddenden.

Monday, 19th July 1971

For the next five weeks, Cranbrook magistrates convened each Monday morning, only to be told that Pankhurst was still unfit to appear before them. Each time he was further remanded in custody for another seven days.

Monday, 23rd August 1971

Pankhurst appeared for just thirty-eight seconds at Cranbrook court. This time the charge included the murder of his five children, as well as his wife. He was supported by prison officers. His empty left sleeve was tucked into the pocket of his grey tweed jacket, and a dressing on the back of his head was held in place by a white surgical net. As before, he was represented by Mr Thomas Hulme. After the hearing, Pankhurst was assisted from the court and taken back by car to Wormwood Scrubs Prison Hospital in London.

Monday, 13th September 1971

Again, after Cranbrook magistrates' hearings had been repeatedly delayed due to Pankhurst's health, he was eventually brought from Wormwood Scrubs to Cranbrook in an unmarked green police van. Several of his relatives were allowed to speak to him in a small room at the front of the courthouse, both before and after the proceedings. For the first time, he walked into the courtroom unaided. Prison warders surrounded the dock during the hearing. Cranbrook magistrates sent Pankhurst for trial at the next Kent Assizes for the murder of his wife and five children. He was granted legal aid. The court's public gallery was full for the six-minute hearing.

Thursday, 4th November 1971

At the Kent Assizes at Maidstone, Dr James Dexter, senior medical officer of Wormwood Scrubs, described Pankhurst as being in a "grossly abnormal state" at the time of committing the alleged offences.

Mr Malcolm Morris QC appeared for Pankhurst and said that in the ordinary course of events, the jury would try a man of charges preferred against him. He said that before a man could be tried for a criminal offence, he must have been able to understand what was going on and must be of sufficient intellect that he could follow the proceedings in court and instruct counsel. If his intellect was such that he could not instruct counsel or follow proceedings, then he was unable to stand his trial. In this supposition, the prosecution did not dispute the position.

Dr Dexter said that Pankhurst had been under his observation in hospital for periods between June and November and outlined his hospital treatment at East Grinstead and in prison. He also told of how Pankhurst had been in hospital again at Hammersmith when he had developed a grave condition of his kidneys. He concluded that, in his opinion, Pankhurst in his present state was unfit to plead to an indictment, instruct counsel, or follow proceedings in court. Dr K. Loucas, a consultant psychiatrist at Broadmoor Hospital, said that he agreed with the doctor's conclusions. Mr Justice Crichton told the jury the evidence was all one way. There was only one conclusion they could reach. There was no challenge that Pankhurst was insane and could not be tried. To this, the jury agreed. The judge ordered that Pankhurst be admitted to a hospital specified by the Secretary of State. In the meantime, the hospital at Wormwood Scrubs would be a place of safety for him.

Tuesday, 16th November 1971

The inquest into the six deaths was adjourned for an indefinite period. No evidence was submitted to the coroner. It was now unlikely that the full story of this most ghastly of crimes would ever be made known to the public.

Late 1971

Pankhurst was taken to Broadmoor high-security psychiatric hospital, Berkshire, under section 65 of the Mental Health Act, 1969. He was to stay there for an indefinite period.

1972

Pankhurst was fitted with an artificial arm but refused to wear it because he did not like it.

Mid 1974

On hearing rumours that Pankhurst might be released from Broadmoor, local residents in Biddenden, Tenterden and surrounding areas raised a petition begging that Pankhurst should remain incarcerated. This was sent to the Home Office with a copy to the Queen.

Early 1975

Dr Edgar Udwin, the senior Broadmoor consultant psychiatrist, considered preparing Pankhurst for a return to normal life.

Mid 1975

Dr Udwin arranged for Pankhurst's transfer to an unnamed open hospital in preparation for his release into the community.

November 1975

A meeting was held between the clinical and social work staff from Broadmoor Hospital, the Bexley Open Psychiatric Hospital, and an officer of the Kent Probation and After-Care Service. They discussed Pankhurst's proposed transfer from Broadmoor to the Kent hospital.

Monday, 29th December 1975

Pankhurst was granted a period of leave from Broadmoor to assist in his rehabilitation and was sent to Bexley Hospital.

Early January 1976

After finding out that Thomas Pankhurst had been released from Broadmoor and placed in an open psychiatric hospital ready for his imminent return to society, *News of the World* reporters laid siege to the close relations of his wife and various government officials, intending to get a nationwide scoop.

Mrs Pankhurst's sister, Mrs Lucy Woolliams, said that she was shocked at the decision, that it was far too early to release Pankhurst, and that when Pankhurst was free, he would be able to marry and have children again. She understood that Pankhurst was to go to live with his mother, who was seventy and was worried about who would look after Pankhurst if anything happened to his mother. Mrs Woolliams' husband, Denis, said that he would be contacting his M.P. to see if there was anything he could do. He also let it be known that he was going to apply for a gun licence and tell the authorities why he wanted it. He was sure some other members of their family would do the same. His wife was anxious, and he wanted to protect his family.

Mr Keith Speed, Conservative M.P. for Ashford, said that he would be making urgent enquiries to the Home Secretary as he thought there had been enough recent cases where released patients had done some pretty awful things and that the authorities must be absolutely sure before anyone is released. After such a short time, he had the gravest doubts about any chap with Pankhurst's recent record being allowed back into society.

Mr Bryant Godman Irvine, Conservative M.P. for Rye and Bexhill, East Sussex, said that he would also be taking up the matter with the Home Secretary.

Government departments, through a spokesman for the Department of Health and Social Security, said that when a patient was moved from hospitals like Broadmoor, it was to prepare them for release. He said that doctors would make their recommendations in these cases to the Home Secretary when they were sure the individual was ready and that Social Services had arranged adequate supervision. They said that Pankhurst was moved to Bexley Hospital under a number of conditions and that he must obey everything his doctors said. If he was allowed out on an excursion, he must not go anywhere near his old home at Biddenden. He could go to Maidstone, where some of his relatives lived, but only with express permission from medical staff. If he disobeyed any restrictions, he would be sent back to Broadmoor.

Sunday, 11th January 1976

Residents living near Bexley Hospital were frightened by the contents of the article splashed across the front page of the *News of the World* containing details of the interviews of the preceding weeks. They were concerned that Pankhurst had been moved to Bexley Hospital and questioned the lax conditions under which he was being held there.

Monday, 12th January 1976

More articles started to appear in the provincial and national press concerning Pankhurst's removal to Bexley and his close proximity to a primary school. There were also concerns amongst the late Mrs Pankhurst's family that Thomas Pankhurst was soon to be released and move in with his 70-year-old mother in Tenterden, just a few miles from the Biddenden home where the murders were committed.

Local M.P.s wrote a letter to Dr Shirley Summerskill, a junior minister at the Home Office, raising issues concerning public safety due to the manner and speed with which Pankhurst was being released back into the community. The minister then made urgent enquiries into the case. In complete contrast, the near relatives of Thomas Pankhurst were more than happy for him to be released as soon as possible. Some of them had even taken him out from Bexley Hospital to go shopping in Lewisham.

Wednesday, 14th January 1976

The headmaster of Maypole Primary School, opposite Bexley Hospital on Dartford Heath, announced that he had taken extra precautions to protect his two hundred and forty pupils from the inmates of the hospital. He said that they would be under constant supervision at school, and parents had been given exact going-home times so they could meet their children and ensure they arrived home safely.

Residents organised a petition to the Home Office demanding the immediate return of Thomas Pankhurst to Broadmoor.

Mr Edward Heath, former Prime Minister and M.P. for Bexley said he was very concerned about the case and was taking the matter up personally with the Home Secretary.

Mrs Janet White, secretary of the Maypole Club (a residents' organisation), said that the people of Bexley felt strongly about the matter because they could not allow their children to go out on the heath without worrying about what would happen to them.

Mr Arun Patel, who ran a sub-post office opposite the hospital, said that he was going to get a petition signed by all the residents in the area and send it to the Home Office with a view to having Pankhurst sent back to the maximum-security hospital at Broadmoor.

A hospital spokesman said that Pankhurst was free to wander in and out of the hospital as he pleased and described him as: "One inoffensive little man."

Monday, 19th January 1976

A mass meeting of 150 parents demanded that greater protection be afforded to their children at Maypole School. They sought a permanent gatekeeper at the open hospital. They had raised this point previously and had never received a satisfactory answer. They also wanted to know if there was a security wing in the hospital and, if so, what sort of patients were there and what offences they had committed.

At their hour-and-a-half-long meeting on Monday night with the headmaster, Mr John Maidwell, and Dartford's Divisional Education Officer, Mr Keith Forward, they were assured that everything had been done to protect their children. They were advised that a welfare assistant employed part-time at the school had increased her hours to give complete supervision of the children inside the school.

She escorted them to the mobile toilet in the school playground and made sure they were never left alone. The school's lollipop lady would be asked to work longer hours so children who were leaving late would be protected outside the school gates. If children were likely to be delayed, parents would be immediately informed. Each child was protected on journeys to and from school.

After the meeting, Mr Maidwell said that they had tried to show parents that they had taken adequate steps to deal with the situation: "It was something we had to look at very closely. The meeting had been constructive, and instead of an emotional response, we now have hard, clinical facts to present to the hospital people when we meet them."

Thursday, 22nd January 1976
The front page of the *Bexleyheath & Welling Observer* contained an exclusive interview with Pankhurst's psychiatrist, who was very clear in his admissions that he was under no illusions that Pankhurst could safely be returned to society.

Doctors originally thought that Pankhurst would be at Bexley for about one or two years, the length of time they felt it would take to rehabilitate him. They did not anticipate him living with his mother in Tenterden. His psychiatrist had said that it seemed sensible to get him placed elsewhere in the community away from the local scene as they did not want him to live near his in-laws again.

Friday, 23rd January 1976

Mr Keith Speed, M.P., put a question in the House of Commons concerning Pankhurst's admission to Bexley Hospital. Mr Roy Jenkins, Home Secretary, responded that the move was to assist in the prisoner's rehabilitation; and that since the admission to Bexley, the hospital social workers had kept in touch with the probation officer.

John Maidwell, Mr Keith Forward, and Mrs Hopley, a parent manager for Maypole School, had a two-hour discussion with senior hospital officials.

Monday, 26th January 1976

Mr Sydney Irving, M.P. for Dartford, had a private meeting at the hospital when he discussed his constituents' fears and the whole question of patient security with hospital officials.

Afterwards, he said that the hospital authorities recognised the problems which arose from patients who might wander out, perhaps in their dressing gowns or pyjamas. They intended to consider staffing at the gates to try to prevent this from happening. They emphasised that they didn't take any patients they regarded as dangerous, but there had been no change in policy in respect of the patients referred to Bexley. In the case of Pankhurst, they believed him to be harmless. They emphasised that if they had believed that there was any danger, they would not have accepted him.

Tuesday, 27th January 1976

An official letter from the school reporting on the meeting of the previous Friday was distributed to parents of children at Maypole School. In it, there were a series of questions raised by parents at their special meeting of the previous week and the associated replies from the hospital.

Parents also posed questions about having a guard at the hospital gates to monitor the patients' comings and goings. They asked the same question a year previously when the suggestion was turned down for financial reasons. This time, the hospital agreed to investigate the possibilities again

Mid-February 1976

Mr Keith Speed M.P. received a reply to his letter to the junior minister at the Home Office stating that medical opinion was that Pankhurst was no danger to others. It was thought that he needed assistance to acclimatise himself to the outside world and that he had at all times been calm and cooperative at Bexley.

Thursday, 4th March 1976

Mr Edward Heath, MP, gave reassurances to residents living near Bexley Hospital, who lived in fear of roaming patients. Mr Heath quoted a letter from the Home Secretary, in which he said that in all such cases, the safety of the public was the paramount consideration.

Mr Heath also consulted Social Service Secretary Mrs Barbara Castle about Pankhurst and the question of patient supervision outside the hospital. She said that in view of the apprehension felt by the local community, including teachers and parents of the Maypole Primary School, the hospital authorities had arranged that Pankhurst would not leave the hospital without an escort.

Mr Heath concluded by saying that he stressed that the future of cases of this kind was fundamentally in the hands of the Home Secretary and that he had left him in no doubt of his constituents' fears. The question of a full-time warden at the Gate Lodge at the entrance to the hospital, raised by the Maypole School parents, was raised by Mr Heath, and Mrs Castle's reply had been that informal patients were at liberty to leave the hospital and could not be turned back at the gate. The question of cost and the desperate need for additional staff had to be taken into account when considering employing a gate porter. The gate lodge was now used by fire prevention officers who had agreed to look out for and turn back any patient dressed in night attire seen leaving the hospital.

A hospital spokesman said that Pankhurst was making good progress. He had been out with his relatives since the publicity about his transfer and was expected to be at Bexley for six months and then transferred to another hospital for further rehabilitation treatment.

After this, nothing more appeared in the provincial press concerning the case of Richard Thomas Pankhurst, so one can only assume that he was safely rehabilitated back into society without further issue, even though it was such a short time since he had been in such a grossly abnormal state that he murdered his wife and all five of their children.

Let it be borne in mind that not even a mere five years had passed since the horrific events at 51 Chulkhurst. This should be compared to Bertha Peterson, who, when she was committed to Broadmoor, was to remain there for the rest of her years with no chance of any reprieve.

Sources

There is a document at the National Archives at Kew (ASSI 36/794) entitled *MURDER: Pankhurst, Richard Thomas*, dated 1971. Disappointingly, this document is 'closed' and cannot be 'opened' until 1st January 2056. No reason is given for its closure.

The British Library

- 19710000 - *East Kent Gazette*
- 19710623 - *Chatham Evening Post*
- 19710624 - *Chatham Evening Post*
- 19710624 - *Daily Mail*
- 19710624 - *Daily Telegraph*
- 19710624 – *London Evening Standard*
- 19710624 - *The Guardian*
- 19710624 - *The Sun*
- 19710625 - *Kent and Sussex Courier*
- 19710625 - *Kent Messenger*
- 19710625 - *Kentish Express*
- 19710630 - *Chatham Evening Post*
- 19710702 - *Kent Messenger*
- 19710702 - *Kentish Express*
- 19710709 - *Kent Messenger*
- 19710713 - *Chatham Evening Post*
- 19710714 - *Chatham Evening Post*
- 19710716 - *Kent Messenger*

- 19710716 - *Kentish Express*

- 19710723 - *Kent Messenger*

- 19710723 - *Kentish Express*

- 19710730 - *Kent Messenger*

- 19710806 - *Kentish Express*

- 19710813 - *Chatham Evening Post*

- 19710820 - *Kent Messenger*

- 19710827 - *Kent & Sussex Courier*

- 19710827 - *Kentish Express*

- 19710827 - *Kent Messenger*

- 19710903 - *Kent Messenger*

- 19710903 - *Kentish Express*

- 19710910 - *Kent Messenger*

- 19710917 - *Kent Messenger*

- 19710917 - *Kent Express*

- 19711105 - *Kent Express*

- 19711117 - *Chatham Evening Post*

- 19711119 - *Kent Messenger*

- 19720000 - *East Kent Gazette*

- 19750000 - *East Kent Gazette*

- 19760000 - *East Kent Gazette*

- 19760111 - *News of the World*

- 19760112 - *Guardian*

- 19760115 - *Bexleyheath & Welling Observer*

- 19760122 - *Bexleyheath & Welling Observer*

- 19760129 - *Bexleyheath & Welling Observer*
- 19760304 - *Bexleyheath & Welling Observer*

The British Newspaper Archive

- 19760112 - *Birmingham Daily Post*
- 19760112 - *Daily Mirror*
- 19760116 - *Aberdeen Evening Express*
- 19760116 - *Kent & Sussex Courier*
- 19760120 - *Daily Mirror*
- 19760130 - *Kent & Sussex Courier*
- 19760220 - *Kent & Sussex Courier*

The Times Archive

- 19710624 - *The Times*
- 19710630 - *The Times*

Websites

- amok.fandom.com/wiki/Thomas_Pankhurst
- www.findagrave.com/cgibin/fg.cgi?page=gr&GRid=123900648
- www.findmypast.co.uk (England & Wales, Births, 1837-2006 and England & Wales, Deaths, 1837-2007)
- www.hansard.millbanksystems.com/writtenanswers/1976/jan/23/broadmoor-patient-leave-of-absence
- www.news.google.com/newspapers (19710623 - *The Evening News*).

Chapter 4 – 1991: Bell

In 1991, a Biddenden resident was involved in a contract killing.

Terrence (Terry) John Daddow (b. 7th November 1939, d. 26th November 1991)

Terry Daddow's birth was recorded at Redruth, Cornwall, in quarter one of 1940. He lived in Chaplefield Cottage, Dixter Lane, Northiam, East Sussex. His first marriage was to Wendy Harris in September 1962 at Falmouth, Cornwall, who reportedly later committed suicide. By a second marriage to Theresa M. Bridges in December 1972 at Banbury, Oxfordshire; he had three sons. His third marriage was to Jean Lillian Blackman.

Jean Lillian Daddow (b. 1940)

Jean Daddow lived in Chaplefield Cottage, Dixter Lane, Northiam, East Sussex and was a hairdresser's assistant in Tenterden. As Jean Brown, her first marriage was to Alan Blackman, with whom she had one son, Roger Blackman. Her second marriage was to Terry Daddow in 1998 at Gretna Green.

Robert Adam Bell (b. 1959)

Robert Bell, a Yorkshireman, lived in Knaves Acre, Headcorn, Kent. He was a former lance corporal in the Transport Corps of the British Army and also served in the Foreign Legion. He was married to Sarah with a daughter, Pip.

Roger Hugh Blackman (b. 1969)

Roger Blackman's birth was recorded at Ashford, Kent, in quarter four of 1969. He lived in Tenterden Road, Biddenden and was a mechanic and small-time drugs dealer. He was the son of Jean Daddow from her first marriage.

The events that were to lead up to this crime and those that resulted from it were as follows:

1979

Terry Daddow was appointed a financial consultant by Lloyds Bank at their branch in Tenterden, Kent.

Jean Blackman had, for a long time, led a lively and permissive life by cheating on her husband with an endless stream of paramours. In an attempt to hide her assignations from her spouse, she frequently installed her lovers into the marital home under the guise of them being lodgers.

1985

Jean was a regular customer at Lloyds Bank, Tenterden. It was here that she met Terry Daddow to discuss the theft of her credit cards. Both being of a rather passionate persuasion, their business relationship soon blossomed into an emotional one. Before long, Terry had moved out of the matrimonial home with his wife, Teresa, and their family, and he and Jean set up home together as lovers.

November 1988

Terry and Jean then moved into a house in Tenterden Road, Biddenden, but found this unsatisfactory as her ex-husband still had access to a workshop at the rear of the property.

There were rumours abroad that Terry had taken advantage of some of his clients at the bank, particularly the elder females with whom he dealt, and that he had dreamed up ideas of blackmailing the old ladies with sexually explicit photos taken after Terry and Jean had laced the pensioners' drinks.

Late 1988

Terry Daddow and Jean Blackman married at Gretna Green.

1989

Not long after their marriage, Jean set about availing herself of Terry's fortune, much of which came from the old ladies they had befriended. Before long she had more than thirty different bank and building society accounts under her control.

May 1990

One of Terry's clients, a 92-year-old widow from Tenterden, provided a gift of a substantial sum of money to help the couple buy their £200,000 Chaplefield Cottage in Dixter Lane, Northiam, East Sussex. The widow, Anne Burton, was president of Tenterden Conservative Club and had been so enamoured by his smooth-talking and financial wizardry that she had agreed to pay for the couple's £160,000 home after they had announced that they were to get married. She also paid a further £40,000 to have it refurbished. Not surprisingly, there were whispers that Terry and Jean had conned the gullible old lady out of her cash. The widow had only agreed to the gift if the Daddows would guarantee that they would not inform her nephews and nieces of the deal. To this, they, of course, agreed.

Mike Pearson, Anne Burton's nephew, made a formal complaint about Terry's behaviour concerning his aunt's financial affairs, alleging that Mrs Burton has been conned into making substantial gifts to the Daddows. After many months of investigation into the matter, Lloyds Bank declared that there had been no underhand dealing and that their employee had had an exemplary record during the twenty years of his employment with them.

May 1991

Using the photographic skills they had developed to blackmail their elderly female benefactors, the Daddows frequently took nude snapshots of one another at their Northiam cottage, and Jean Daddow often got turned on when her husband wrote kinky letters to her.

As more reports arrived on the desks of the management of Lloyds Bank in Tenterden concerning Terry's behaviour with his more elderly female clients, it was decided that he was to be ordered to take early retirement on health grounds. It was conjectured locally that, as he was now to spend most of his time in their Northiam cottage, Jean would find it more awkward to continue her extra-marital affairs with her long string of lovers.

Terry subsequently set himself up as a freelance financial advisor to enable him to continue his dubious dealings with the elderly of the area.

Summer 1991

Jean Daddow and Roger Blackman had grown to hate Terry Daddow and decided that it was time that they got rid of him. She had considered divorce but was worried about the financial implications that might occur if they did split up. Roger hated him because of his attitude towards his mother. He had found reason, on a number of occasions, to go to their cottage to sort out arguments between the couple.

Robert Bell had an addiction to cannabis, and Roger Blackman was his supplier. Bell had amassed debts of over £5,000 to Blackman, who was now looking for repayment. Bell was out of work and broke and was desperate to settle his debts. Being of ex-military stock, Bell appeared to be the ideal candidate to carry out the dirty work for Jean and her son.

Mrs Daddow withdrew £11,000 in cash from one of the couple's few remaining joint accounts at Lloyds Bank in Rye, East Sussex, loading all the money into her handbag. Her son then added a further £1,000 cash to this and roughly arranged all the money into a dozen bundles and placed them into an old shoebox. In Blackman's garage, at his home in Tenterden Road, Biddenden, having explained their requirements to Bell, they handed over the box with its contents to their newly recruited hitman and waited for events to unfold.

Before long Bell realised that he had bitten off more than he could chew and quickly lost all interest in being a paid hitman. He had no intention of going through with the murder, despite agreeing to it during their meeting. He tried to placate Blackman, who had already threatened to harm Bell's family if he did not progress further with their plans. Despite Bell's uncertainty about his role in the conspiracy, the trio regularly met during the summer and autumn of 1991, plotting variously to shoot, poison, batter, run-down or car bomb Terry Daddow.

October 1991
Their preparations were followed by a series of failed attempts on Terry Daddow's life. In the first attempt, Blackman gave Bell a crash helmet and a piece of steel piping and told him to murder Terry. Jean Daddow left the back door of their Northiam cottage open to let Bell creep in. She even moved ornaments that might have got in his way. Bell made his way in but, unfortunately, was heard by Terry, who grabbed an axe and frightened him off. In a subsequent attack, Bell stalked Terry Daddow around Devon, where he was on holiday, but failed to shoot him as planned. Another proposed ambush of Daddow, on one of his favourite walks,

failed too. Added to this, Blackman was continuously supplying his mother with small amounts of recreational drugs, which she added to Terry's meals in powdered form, causing him to hallucinate and suffer from depression. Her son found this part of their degradation of Terry Daddow rather amusing.

Later, Bell actually met Terry Daddow face-to-face by posing as a conservationist from the Badger Protection Society and appeared at their doorstep armed with nothing more than a clipboard and a small package supplied by Blackman. Bell surreptitiously passed the package to Jean out of sight of her husband, who, in turn, emptied its contents into Terry's coffee. It contained a crushed mixture of amphetamine sulphate and ecstasy tablets. After drinking the noxious concoction, Terry became extremely ill but eventually survived this attempt on his life.

Tuesday, 5th November 1991
Terry Daddow, on advice from his wife, changed his will by removing his bequests to his three sons and directing them to herself: a move that, in the event of his death, would benefit her to the tune of over £300,000.

Tuesday, 26th November 1991

Morning: Terry Daddow placed the following notice in the personal section of the small ads of the *Wealden Advertiser*: *"DADDOW, TERRY, JEAN. Because of malicious gossip would like it known they are happily married and together. All have been proved by solicitors etc. NOT guilty of fraud, theft or senility. Thanks to the few true friends who believed in us perhaps the rest could find themselves to criticize or work for their sick minds."*

The woman who took down the advertisement in the newspaper office thought it very strange and checked with her managing director to confirm it was acceptable to print the notice.

20.30: A man, six-foot-tall, was seen in Ewhurst Lane, Northiam. He was in his 40s with greying hair and a cropped beard and was wearing a green zipped-up Barbour jacket, blue jeans and gloves. He asked for directions and didn't seem to know his way around the village.

22.30: Mike Pearson was drinking in The Vine Inn, Tenterden, with, amongst others, the former Assistant Chief Constable of Kent.

Terry Daddow left his bedroom to open the front door to a mysterious late-night caller to their Northiam cottage. While he did this, Jean was preparing for bed. She was about to take a pill when she heard a shout which she did not recognise as Terry's voice. There was then an horrendous bang at almost the same time. Terry's attacker had let loose with a twelve-bore shotgun directly into his heart, killing him instantly. While the gunman made his getaway, Jean came out of the bathroom and looked over the bannisters. She could see Terry lying there and went downstairs, where she could see he was bleeding slightly from his mouth. In shock, she sat on the stairs, talking to him.

22.45: Jean Daddow eventually dialled 999 to raise the alarm. Some of her neighbours were aware that there had been a not inconsiderable gap between hearing the gunshot and the arrival of the emergency services.

One of the first police officers to arrive on the scene was P.C. Anthony Smith, who sat with Jean, trying to find out the identity of her husband's killer. He found her in tears, but she was easily comforted.

Wednesday, 27th November 1991

When asked by the police why she had delayed calling them and the medics, she said that she was just not thinking straight. She also told them that she thought she had seen a man, whom she recognised as Mrs Anne Burton's nephew, Mike Pearson, running away from the cottage. She went on to say that she had long suspected her husband of being unfaithful to her and that the perpetrator of the crime may have been an associate of one of his mistresses.

07.18: Eighteen armed police surrounded Mike Pearson's family home at the Rolvenden end of Tenterden High Street to arrest him and his two sons. The police made a telephone call to Pearson, and the voice of Superintendent David Hatcher told him the house was surrounded by armed officers. All three Pearsons were arrested and taken to Hastings Police Station for questioning.

The local police instituted door-to-door enquiries in Northiam but ended up with little to show for their efforts. Whilst this was taking place, other members of the constabulary started investigations into the private and commercial lives of the victim and his wife.

Thursday, 28th November 1991
Having been in the company of an ex-police officer at the time the crime was committed, Mike Pearson and his two sons were released without charge.

Saturday, 30th November 1991

Detective Superintendent Brian Foster, who led the investigation, made an appeal to the public for information concerning the gossip about Mr Daddow and his wife, which would appear to have been circulating in Tenterden. He said that they were anxious to speak to anyone who had had dealings with Mr and Mrs Daddow, whether they were social or financial. Every call was to be treated in complete confidence. It was not long before the police nicknamed their inquiries the 'Terry and June case' after the TV sitcom couple.

Anne Burton, being very upset at the arrest of her nephew, Mike Pearson, after Jean Daddow's accusations, visited the wife of the deceased and tackled her over the claim. Mrs Daddow denied that she had implicated Mr Pearson and told his aunt that she had seen nothing because she was in the bath at the time Terry Daddow had been shot. Later the *Kentish Express* begged the very observant question that, if she had been in the bath, how could she have given a description of the killer?

December 1991

Realising that the police were starting to make enquiries about him, Robert Bell flew to the United States in an attempt to put a good distance between himself and his pursuers. Whilst there, Bell telephoned the London Office of *The Sun* and talked to journalist Paul Hooper. He told Hooper that the shotgun killing of Terry Daddow was linked by drugs to a second gruesome murder where a headless, handless body was found on the A23, London to Brighton road. He said that if police knew the link, they would crack the biggest drug ring in the southeast of England. He claimed that Mr Daddow was a money launderer for drug dealers who had bumped him off for talking too much. He also said that he knew the police wanted to question him but that he could be jailed for ten years if he returned to England. Bell was very insistent on his innocence and told Hooper that he hadn't murdered anyone. Hooper then asked Bell about the second murder, and Bell said there was a German connection and that he knew the identity of the torso.

Monday, 2nd December 1991
Twenty-five uniformed officers continued their house-to-house inquiries. The search for clues moved to ditches and farmland around Northiam.

Monday, 9th December 1991
At a press conference in Hastings Police Station, Jean Daddow directed an appeal to the people of Tenterden and Biddenden. She begged anyone with information to come forward and to tell the police of any dealings they had had

with Terry Daddow. The widow was making her first public comment since the murder. She said that she could think of no reason for the shooting. She dismissed the theory that it had something to do with Mr Daddow's financial dealings, though she did admit that a 91-year-old woman had bought them their house as a gift but said her husband had been cleared of any fraud.

She went on to say that her husband had been accused, within his work, of persuading old ladies to leave him their money and that it wasn't true. Mrs Daddow said she and her husband had been upset by gossip about their marriage, which had been circulating in Biddenden and Tenterden. She declared that theirs was a happy marriage. Mrs Daddow also told how her husband had been under treatment for anxiety and so had not recently been working as a financial consultant. In her role as the grieving widow, Jean suggested that her husband's killer was a jealous husband or boyfriend taking action as a result of one of his affairs.

At the conference, Detective Chief Inspector Snelling said police had now ruled Mr Pearson out of the inquiry but still had an open mind about the killing. By this stage, police had interviewed nearly five hundred people.

January 1992

Terry Daddow's killer had still not been apprehended despite an intensive police investigation involving fifty detectives, although police were still anxious to eliminate two men seen in Northiam on the night of the murder.

Tuesday, 28th January 1992

10.00: Jean Daddow and Roger Blackman were arrested and interviewed at Hastings Police Station. Detective Inspector Kevin Moore described this as a positive line of inquiry.

Wednesday, 29th January 1992

Evening: The mother and son were questioned for thirty-two hours before being released on police bail until April.

Early March 1992

Detective Superintendent Brian Foster made a personal telephone call to Bell in Canada, asking him to come back to answer questions. He let it be known that they could have him picked up by the FBI and forcibly returned to Britain, if necessary. Bell, who had once conned car giants Nissan into giving him a £50,000-a-year job after convincing them he had a computer degree, thought he could talk his way out of the murder, but he was wrong.

Wednesday, 4th March 1992

15.30: Bell returned to England and was met by detectives at the airport, who immediately arrested and charged him with murder. He said that Blackman was with him at the time of the shooting, that he had wavered and that it was Jean's son who had grabbed the gun and pulled the trigger. He claimed that Blackman had provided the gun and that the whole plot had been dreamed up by Jean Daddow, and that he had been reluctant to kill anyone.

In his interview with police, Bell gave officers the essential details about the months leading up to the murder. These details were to be crucial in the forthcoming trial, for without them, detectives later admitted, it would have been almost impossible to mount a prosecution.

Friday, 6th March 1992

Detectives turned up at Jean Daddow's parents' house in Biddenden with a view to arresting her, but on arrival, they found her comatose on the settee, suffering from a suspected drug overdose. She was rushed to Maidstone District Hospital and was later transferred to the William Harvey Hospital in Ashford. Her condition was described as 'serious'.

Roger Blackman was arrested.

Magistrates granted detectives an extra thirty-six hours to continue questioning Robert Bell.

Saturday, 7th March 1992

Roger Blackman appeared before Hastings Magistrates' Court and was charged with conspiracy to murder. Robert Bell also appeared in the court and was charged with Terry Daddow's murder and conspiracy to murder. Both men were remanded in custody to appear before the court again on Monday 16th March.

Tuesday, 10th March 1992

15.30: Jean Daddow was released from the hospital, immediately arrested, and driven to Hastings Police Station.

22.24: Jean Daddow was charged with conspiracy to murder her husband.

Wednesday, 11th March 1992

Jean Daddow appeared at Hastings Magistrates' Court and was remanded in custody to appear at the court again on the following Monday.

Monday, 16th March 1992

Jean Daddow and the two men were accused of plotting the killing at Headcorn between June and 27th November 1991. All three appeared before Hastings magistrates and were remanded in custody until 13th April.

Monday, 23rd March 1992

At Lewes Crown Court, Jean Daddow was conditionally released on bail on the advice of the judge in chambers. The conditions were that she lived in Biddenden, reported to Cranbrook Police Station once a week, and did not interfere with any of the witnesses. The two men accused of the plot remained in custody.

Monday, 12th April 1992

Lawyers were given four weeks to study the evidence. Hastings magistrates heard that transcripts of the interviews with detectives ran to 1,100 pages and that extra time was needed to examine them. Bell and Blackman were further remanded in custody until 11th May.

Wednesday, 1st July 1992

After a two-day committal hearing, Hastings magistrates sent the three accused for trial at Lewes Crown Court. Subsequently, magistrates bailed Jean Daddow and ordered her to remain living in the family home in Northiam. Bell and Blackman remained in custody.

Thursday, 12th November 1992

Whilst on remand in C-wing at Lewes Prison, Blackman attempted to get another inmate to murder Bell by lacing his drugs with poison. He suggested that the attempt should be carried out on the anniversary of Terry Daddow's death to make it look like Bell had committed suicide through remorse. Blackman was unable to carry out the deed as Bell was by then in another prison because of the problems he had with Blackman. Blackman told the other inmate that if Bell didn't appear in court to give evidence, then he (Blackman) would be able to walk free. Fortunately, the police got to hear of the plot and managed to move Bell elsewhere.

Detective Superintendent Brian Foster later said that if Blackman's plot to kill Bell had been successful, it would have been the end of the investigation. It was fortunate that they got to hear about it and managed to move them to different prisons. But it showed how important Bell's confession was and the extreme lengths to which Blackman was prepared to go.

Wednesday, 24th February 1993

The trial of the three plotters began at Hove Crown Court, East Sussex. Bell was charged with murder and conspiracy to murder, and Robert Blackman and Jean Daddow with conspiracy to murder. All three pleaded not guilty.

Prosecutor Mr Camden Pratt said that the plot to kill Terry Daddow had been hatched during the summer of 1991 and that as far as Bell was concerned, he had no personal grudge against Terry Daddow. It was purely a contract killing, and it became clear from police investigations that, according to Mrs Daddow, there had been a degree of physical violence from Mr Daddow towards her and that this looked likely to be a motive for the crime. Mr Pratt also said that Mrs Daddow had been seen with black eyes and bruising. She had needed money to pay off the hitman and withdrew £11,000 from the couple's joint account at Lloyds.

The prosecution continued by telling how Bell had fled to America in the middle of the murder investigation and had been interviewed by detectives on his return. Bell told police that the suggestion was that Terry Daddow had to be got rid of so that the family did not lose any of the property or the money they had. It had got to the stage where he was offered £12,000 to assist in the killing of Terry Daddow. He thought at the time this could be a way of clearing his debts, but he didn't think Terry would end up being killed. At the last minute, he lost his nerve, and Blackman did it.

Thursday, 4th March 1993

Roger Blackman's former girlfriend, Rachel Carmichael, told the court that Jean said that Terry used to get drunk occasionally and hit her. She had seen her with bruises on her face and arms. Roger did not like Terry and was upset about his parents splitting up and blamed it on Terry. Jean's main complaint about Terry was that he was out late at night because of work, and then he would drink when he came in. She once said she did not like Terry and wanted him out of her life. She wanted to know if Roger knew anybody who would kill Terry for about £1,000. He said he knew people who would just do it for fun, and she could keep the money. She said it was a silly idea, and he just laughed and dismissed it.

A neighbour of the Daddows, Mrs Angela Singer, a dental receptionist, also told the court that Jean came round to her house on one occasion. She said her husband was depressed and had had a few drinks. He had hit her, and she thought he had thrown something at her. At times, she said she had enough, but she felt a lot for him. She felt as if she could not put up with him anymore, but she felt that things were getting better. She said that he would not let her leave. Mrs

Singer then told the jury that she had heard the shot that killed Mr Daddow.

Wednesday, 10th March 1993

The court heard that Jean Daddow had told the police that she had discovered an unused condom, two months after the murder, in a cassette case in the couple's Proton car. She said that she thought the contraceptive was her husband's and that he had been having an affair. This disclosure had sent detectives on a new line of inquiry, but the prosecution claimed the story of an affair was set up as a red herring by Mrs Daddow to throw them off the scent of the real killer.

Thursday, 11th March 1993

The court was told of Bell's flight to America and his subsequent return after the involvement of *The Sun* journalist.

Wednesday, 17th March 1993

Hove Crown Court heard evidence from a Mr X who was challenged by Blackman to murder Bell when all three were incarcerated in Lewes Prison.

Thursday, 18th March 1993

In a statement to police, read to the court, Mrs Daddow said the changes to Terry Daddow's will were made after her husband had an argument with his ex-wife, Theresa. She said it was a verbal agreement between Terry and herself and that she would still see to it that his sons got a share.

An 81-year-old widow, Hildegarde Sykes, of Swiss Cottage, Rolvenden Hill, admitted to the court that she was deceived into lending Terry Daddow £25,000 and at one stage planned to leave her cottage to him. She said that Terry had considerable charm and a gift for making everything sound so sad and unfortunate and that she was very fond of him. She felt he was an adopted son and was completely deceived. She thought she was on the ball and alert. It made her feel an awful clot to be deceived so outrageously. She also stated that she had asked him to be her executor and was due to leave her nineteenth-century cottage to him. She explained that shortly before his death, she changed her will and that Jean Daddow had subsequently banned communication with her. She said she was deceived by him until the day he died. She had planned to meet the Daddows to discuss the situation over the will, but before they had a chance to meet, Mr Daddow had been murdered.

Mrs Sykes went on to say that she knew he was an alcoholic, so she never offered him a drink. Sometimes she found the sherry bottle empty after he had called. She lent him the money when he was very keen to take legal action because of unsatisfactory builders, but he said he could not afford it. When he said it would cost £10,000, she was shocked and so was her bank. She took his advice on investments and had every confidence in him. She did not know that the Daddows had been given £160,000 by Mrs Burton to buy their Northiam cottage. Terry Daddow had told her that his uncle had put up the cash.

Wednesday, 24th March 1993

Bell told the jury of his meeting at Blackman's home. He said that Blackman said he could earn money that would not have to be repaid if he was to assist him and his mother in the killing of Terry Daddow. Mrs Daddow had shown him the money at Blackman's house. He had agreed to their faces to go along with it, but he had never had any intention for it to actually go ahead.

Wednesday, 31st March 1993

Jean Daddow broke down in tears as she told the court of the drunken beatings her husband gave her and about the night he was killed. Mrs Daddow denied any involvement in the death or taking part in any plot. She still wore her wedding ring and said that she was besotted with her husband despite the violence. She said that the beatings were sparked by depression caused by an acrimonious divorce from his former wife, Teresa. She said that he suffered a lot from depression. It was a sort of anxiety state brought on by aggravation from his first wife. He started drinking heavily, which made the depression worse. Eventually, she persuaded him to go to the doctors, and he then started getting treatment.

Thursday, 8th April 1993

At Hove Crown Court, after more than eight and a half hours' deliberation, the three perpetrators were found guilty by a unanimous verdict. Mr Justice Hidden convicted Jean Daddow for hiring a contract killer to shoot her husband and conspiracy to murder; Roger Blackman for conspiracy to murder; and Robert Bell for murder and conspiracy to murder. Neither Jean Daddow nor her son showed a flicker of emotion as the jury returned its verdicts. Bell just shook his head. Mr Hidden remanded all three in custody for three weeks and warned them that they faced very long fixed-term sentences or life imprisonment.

After the verdicts were announced, Detective Superintendent Brian Foster said that it was the likelihood that Mrs Daddow had married her husband with murder in mind.

Wednesday, 19th May 1993

Mr Justice Hidden, sentencing at the Old Bailey, told the three conspirators that they put their heads together to conceive and carry out a killing which was cold-blooded and as callous as can be imagined.

Jean Daddow was jailed for eighteen years. She showed no emotion as she was led to the cells. Roger Blackman received a similar sentence. Robert Bell was jailed for life for murder with a recommendation he serve at least fifteen years. He was also sentenced to serve eighteen years concurrently for conspiracy to murder.

Late May 1993

The family of Anne Burton put a block on the sale of the Daddows' cottage and started civil court action.

Wednesday, 27th July 1994

In the north London high-security jail at Wormwood Scrubs, Robert Bell married a prison clerk who he met in the prison officers' mess where he was a cook. Prison chiefs gave Barbara Eggert, who dabbled in the occult, an ultimatum to stop the relationship or face being disciplined. She ignored the no-fraternisation orders and revealed she was going to marry Bell. She was suspended but later decided to resign. Nicknamed *The Witch of Wormwood Scrubs*, Miss Eggert wore a black and red wedding dress for the bizarre ceremony. A dozen friends and workmates attended the hastily arranged service performed by an official from Hammersmith and Fulham Register Office. The marriage was blessed by a Church of England clergyman, the Rev. Gerald Stevenson. After the formalities, the newlywed couple cut a black wedding cake complete with occult symbols.

Head of Security at the Scrubs, Gareth Davies, said a relationship between staff and prisoners was unprofessional and posed a security risk. But a spokesman for the Prison Officers' Association said that it was a fact of life men and women are attracted to each other. Those laws of nature appear in prison as well; where there's a will, there's a way. The mess was a large area, and staff did not patrol it, so he could only presume that the relationship had been consummated there.

Tuesday, 7th November 1995
Jean Daddow was refused leave to appeal against her 18-year jail sentence for conspiracy to murder. Lord Justice Rose rejected her claim of diminished responsibility.

Sunday, 7th March 1999

The following article appeared in *Scotland on Sunday*:

"One of Britain's biggest banks is set to face embarrassing questions over its failure to compensate victims of fraud and blackmail by one of its employees. Campaigners are to target Lloyds TSB's annual meeting in Edinburgh next month on behalf of 86-year-old Clara Hooper and other victims of the so-called Black Horse fraudster, Terry Daddow.

"The financial advisor with Lloyds Bank fleeced elderly women in southern England in the late 1980s and early 1990s. He had pornographic pictures of some victims. His wife, Jean, joined him....Lloyds paid compensation to at least one of Daddow's victims. Others however, received nothing."

"Hooper, from Kent, handed over nearly £23,000 to the fraudster. After the murder she sued for compensation against his estate, but he died penniless and it was too late to sue Lloyds, which had merged with the TSB. Now Hooper's nephew, Charles, has organised a group of protesters, from as far apart as Bath and Dunbartonshire, who will attend the Lloyds TSB meeting at the Edinburgh International Conference Centre and ask what one campaigner called awkward questions. Hooper, 51, said: 'We have been trying for years to get an apology and compensation for Clara, and this campaign reflects my

indignation about how a bank can get too powerful for people to challenge."

Sources

- *The Mammoth Book of Bizarre Crimes*
- *Real Life Crimes*, Volume 8, Part 108
- 19911126 - *Wealden Advertiser*

The British Library

- 19911127 - *Evening Standard*
- 19911129 - *Daily Telegraph*
- 19911129 - *Kent Messenger*
- 19911129 - *Kentish Express*
- 19911130 - *Daily Mail*
- 19911205 - *Kentish Express*
- 19911212 - *Kentish Express*
- 19911219 - *Kentish Express*
- 19920102 - *Kentish Express*
- 19920117 - *Kent & Sussex Courier*
- 19920123 - *Kentish Express*
- 19920130 - *Kentish Express*
- 19920131 - *Kent & Sussex Courier*
- 19920206 - *Kentish Express*
- 19920306 - *Kent & Sussex Courier*
- 19920312 - *Kentish Express*

- 19920313 - *Kent & Sussex Courier*
- 19920313 - *Kent Messenger*
- 19920319 - *Kentish Express*
- 19920320 - *Kent Messenger*
- 19920326 - *Kentish Express*
- 19920416 - *Kent Messenger*
- 19920416 - *Kentish Express*
- 19920702 - *Kentish Express*
- 19920724 - *Kent & Sussex Courier*
- 19930225 - *Kentish Express*
- 19930228 - *Kent & Sussex Courier*
- 19930303 - *Kent & Sussex Courier*
- 19930311 - *Kentish Express*
- 19930312 - *Kent & Sussex Courier*
- 19930318 - *Kentish Express*
- 19930319 - *Kent & Sussex Courier*
- 19930325 - *Kentish Express*
- 19930401 - *Kentish Express*
- 19930409 - *Daily Star*
- 19930415 - *Kentish Express*
- 19930416 - *Kent & Sussex Courier*
- 19990307 - *Scotland on Sunday*.

The British Newspaper Archive

- 19911128 - *Daily Mirror*
- 19911129 - *Dundee Courier*

- 19911130 - *Aberdeen Press and Journal*

- 19911210 - *Dundee Courier*

- 19930227 - *Sandwell Evening Mail*

- 19940731 - Sunday Mirror

- 19940805 - *Hammersmith & Shepherds Bush Gazette*

- 19951108 - *Aberdeen Press and Journal.*

Websites

- www.findmypast.co.uk (England & Wales, Deaths, 1837-2007, England & Wales, Births, 1837-2006 and the National Burial Index for England & Wales Transcription

- www.heraldscotland.com/news 19930226 - *The Herald (Scotland)*

- www.independent.co.uk/news/uk 19930408 - *The Independent*

- www.independent.co.uk/news/uk 19930519 - *The Independent*

- www.totalcrime.co.uk/2014/06/21/murderbook-1900-1999/

Chapter 5 – 2016: Smith and Love

2016 saw a brutal attack on a pensioner in his Biddenden cottage.

Roy Blackman (b. 1942, d. 20th March 2016)

Roy Blackman's birth was registered at Ashford, Kent, in quarter two of 1942. He lived at Heartsay Bungalow, Headcorn Road, Biddenden. He was a well-known and revered widowed pensioner who ran several businesses in the area, including a burger van and a car repair company. He was also an expert bird breeder. A family statement found in the *Daily Telegraph* of 2nd May 2016 recorded that: "He has grafted all his life and was a kind, wise and private man who loved the countryside and his collection of pheasants, ducks and geese." His marriage to Eileen Rolfe was recorded in quarter three of 1966 at Ashford, Kent, as a result of which they had three daughters and a grandchild.

To the best of the author's knowledge, there is no connection between Roy Blackman and Roger Hugh Blackman referred to in the preceding chapter.

Mark Love (b. 1978)

Mark Love's birth was recorded at Tonbridge, Kent, in quarter two of 1978. He lived in Frittenden Road,

Staplehurst, Kent, and was a part-time mechanic and a father-of-four. At the time of these events, he was suffering from depression as a result of the break-up of his marriage.

William (Curly Bill) Smith (b. 1980 d. 1st May 2016)
William Smith was born in Pembury, Kent, and was a traveller who gave his address as Tenterden Road, Golford near Cranbrook. He was a builder by trade and was married to Nancy. They had four children.

The events that were to lead up to this crime and those that resulted from it were as follows:

Sunday, 21st February 2016
A group of four men dressed in black smashed their way into the house of champion clay pigeon shooter George Digweed at Ewhurst Lane, Northiam. They tied up and assaulted Digweed and his wife and stole about £10,000 in cash, two guns and a Toyota Hilux luxury pick-up.

Neighbours reported seeing a dark-coloured Mini Cooper, parked dangerously, near the house.

Monday, 7th March 2016
The Toyota Hilux stolen in the Northiam burglary was found abandoned in Biddenden.

Monday, 21st March 2016

01.00 – 03.00: Roy Blackman interrupted a gang of burglars who broke into his home and subsequently punched, kicked and stamped on him. He was attacked so ferociously that he was left with boot prints on his face and buttocks. He also suffered a brain haemorrhage and multiple fractures to his cheekbone and ribs. The intruders left Mr Blackman for dead and then ransacked his house, turning it into an utter imbroglio as they searched for valuables.

Once they realised that Roy Blackman was dead, the offenders made efforts to destroy any forensic evidence that may have connected them to the crime. They attempted to achieve this by cutting off all the clothing from their victim's body and putting it in a bath full of water. They also used cleaning products to try to wash his bloodstains from the walls of the cottage.

They made off with a large mustard-coloured metal safe, which was about five feet high, two feet wide and two feet deep. The safe was estimated to contain a quarter of a million pounds in cash. Firearms and jewellery were also stolen.

The same dark-coloured Mini Cooper, that was seen at the robbery in Northiam a month earlier was seen nearby.

Morning: One of Roy Blackman's daughters, Nicola, turned up for work at her father's business and discovered his battered body lying naked on his back in the ransacked cottage.

08.57: Police were called to Heartsay Bungalow, where forensic detectives from the Kent and Essex Serious Crime Directorate worked all day at the scene. Police scene-of-crime officers detected Mark Love's DNA in a work glove and on a tap in the upstairs bathroom. The DNA of William Smith was also found on a bottle of cleaning fluid in the lounge.

Later, Detective Inspector Lee Whitehead, who led the investigations, asked for the public's assistance by reporting any suspicious activity they might have seen in the area.

Afternoon: Mark Love and William Smith went on a flash and lavish shopping expedition at the Ashford Designer Outlet loaded with cash stolen from Roy Blackman. The pair visited several shops and spent more than £600 in Fred Perry. In another shop, they bought some clothes and paid with a wad of £20 notes peeled from a bundle. They gave the sales assistant too much cash, and she returned some of the money. She had never seen so much money at one time and thought it was all very unusual. Love asked another shop assistant to get rid of the clothes he had come dressed in and, having changed into the ones he had just bought, he then asked if they had any socks, which the assistant thought to be rather strange as she could not see anything wrong with the ones that he was wearing.

After they left the store, they waited outside in their van. Because of their behaviour, one of the shop assistants suspected them of drink-driving and called the police. The men then went into another store, Lyle & Scott, where Love tried on a jumper and paid for it. He then left behind the Fred Perry jumper he had just purchased in the previous shop. Hidden closed-circuit TV cameras recorded Smith changing his clothes in the toilets at the shopping centre.

Love and Smith then went into a betting shop in Beaver Lane and gambled £140 on a gaming machine. On leaving the betting shop, they were apprehended by the police concerning the alleged drink-driving. As the police could find no evidence of this, the two were allowed to go on their way.

Tuesday, 22nd March 2016
The *post mortem* examination of Roy Blackman revealed that he died as a result of multiple blunt force injuries to the head, neck, chest and abdomen.

Detective Inspector Lee Whitehead said that Mr Blackman had been beaten to death in his own home in what appeared to be an extremely violent burglary. The safe was missing from the property, and they were very keen to locate it. He believed that several suspects had carried out the crime and that they had targeted a vulnerable man in his own home, leaving a trail of devastation in their wake. He went on to say that it was important that the perpetrators were arrested, and he urged anyone who had any information to come forward without delay.

The police also appealed for help in identifying a group of workmen seen at the entrance to a field near Mr Blackman's home on the A274 on Sunday, 20th March. The men were all wearing hi-vis jackets and white hard hats. On the same day, at around 9.40 pm, a man was seen walking along the road near the victim's home.

Wednesday, 23rd March 2016
Early hours: Police swooped on land just off Tenterden Road, in the hamlet of Golford, near Cranbrook. Two men were arrested on suspicion of murder. The suspects, both aged 36 and from Cranbrook, remained in custody. Police spent all morning removing items from the site at Golford.

Morning: Detectives carried out more enquiries, in the neighbourhood of Mr Blackman's cottage, in an effort to identify any witnesses to the crime. Officers were particularly keen to speak to anyone who might have been in the area of Headcorn Road between Weeks Lane and Frittenden Road from 7.30 pm on the Sunday evening to the early hours of the following Monday morning.

Evening: A 49-year-old man was arrested on suspicion of murder and bailed pending further enquiries until Thursday 28th April.

Thursday, 24th March 2016

Detectives searched the abandoned industrial site of Valdene Business Park, on Headcorn Road, near Sutton Valence, about eight miles to the north of Biddenden.

Friday, 25th March 2016

During the afternoon, a family walking along Dig Dog Lane near Cranbrook discovered two firearms, some jewellery and a car registration plate belonging to the dark-coloured Mini Cooper, in a stream. They also discovered a key ring from Roy Blackman Motors.

Thursday, 31st March 2016

A dark-coloured Mini Cooper, displaying cloned registration number plates, was discovered.

Thursday, 7th April 2016

Mark Love presented himself at Folkestone Police Station and was arrested. As a result, police searched Love's lock-up at Pork Pie Farm, about three and a half miles north of Cranbrook. Here they found his van, which was dripping wet and had contained pools of dirty water which had been used in an attempt to remove any forensic evidence that may have been concealed therein. Police believed that it was this van that was used to take away Roy Blackman's safe on the night of his murder.

Saturday, 9th April 2016

Officers arrested a 41-year-old man from the Maidstone area in connection with the murder. He was released on bail pending further enquiries until 1st July.

Sunday, 10th April 2016

Mark Love appeared before Medway Magistrates' Court and was charged with the murder of Roy Blackman and the aggravated burglary of his bungalow. His DNA had been matched to that on a club hammer, and Taser left behind at the Northiam burglary and also on items found at Roy Blackman's house.

Detectives released a picture of a firearm resembling the one reported missing from Mr Blackman's address. They were keen to locate the BSA SuperTen air rifle, which had a laser sight attached to the top.

Monday, 25th April 2016

Police officers, supported by armed units and a helicopter, raided a property at Grants Road, St. Michael's, near Tenterden. No arrests were made.

Evening: Police swooped on a vehicle travelling on the A28 Tenterden Road and arrested a man on suspicion of assisting an offender.

Thursday, 28th April 2016

Police issued an appeal for information on the whereabouts of William Smith, who had earlier been released on bail but was now missing.

Richard Edmondson, who owned Edmondson Interiors in Smiths Lane, Goudhurst, noticed some activity in the lane in an area that he described as just a field. He saw a few people there and a couple of ponies on the land, which was unusual.

The Goudhurst parish council website noted that vehicles had been seen parked in front of a waterworks on the edge of the village. The lay-by had a clear view of a caravan and shack on the land, which had been owned by the Smith family for the past fifteen years.

Sunday, 1st May 2016

20.30: Armed police officers turned up at a Crowbourne Orchard in Smiths Lane. In a planned operation, William Smith was fatally injured when two police officers shot him twice each. He was shot in the head and chest. It was rumoured that Smith was shot near a traveller's site in the area, but this was not confirmed. The Independent Police Complaints Commission rapidly started investigating the incident and carried out tests on what appeared to be non-police firearms that were found at the scene. The guns turned out to be those stolen from George Digweed in the Northiam burglary.

Monday, 2nd May 2016

The area around Smiths Lane remained cordoned off as police forensic officers continued their investigations.

Wednesday, 18th May 2016

Roy Blackman's funeral took place at St. Michael's Church, Smarden. His coffin arrived on the back of one of his own recovery trucks. About 100 mourners attended the service. Police officers were outside the church to provide reassurance.

Wednesday, 1st June 2016

Hundreds of mourners attended William Smith's funeral at St. George's Church, Benenden. After the service, his coffin was taken in a horse-drawn carriage, which led to a procession containing ten limousines and a number of trucks laden with floral tributes and photographs. The cortege headed towards Sissinghurst, passing down Cranbrook High Street to the cemetery in Golford Road. A Kent Police spokesman said that the funeral of William Smith was a private event for the family and that there was no plan for a police presence in the area. Many pubs in the vicinity were shut for the day for fear of trouble breaking out amongst the mourners.

Tuesday, 13th September 2016

Love went on trial at Maidstone Crown Court, accused of both murdering the 73-year-old garage owner and of the aggravated burglary at the home of George and Kate Digweed. Prosecutor Simon Taylor alleged that the recently deceased William Smith was also part of the gang involved in both offences.

Tuesday, 29th September 2016

At the end of the three-week trial, Mark Love appeared wearing a grey blazer, white shirt and dark blue jumper and was flanked by two security guards. He was found guilty of the murder of Roy Blackman and of a separate charge of aggravated burglary at the home of the Digweeds.

Love was sentenced to be imprisoned for life, with a minimum term of twenty-eight years before parole would be considered. He was also sentenced to twelve years for aggravated burglary, to run concurrently with the life term. He showed no emotion when the guilty verdicts were read out nor when the sentences were handed down.

Chief Crown Prosecutor for the Criminal Prosecution Service South East, Jaswant Narwal, said that it was clear from the evidence that Love was part of a group that carefully planned both burglaries well in advance, identifying properties which they knew were likely to contain significant quantities of cash. One was a terrifying ordeal for a couple in their own home, while the other led to the tragic death of a quiet and private man who was the victim of a violent and brutal attack. The level of violence had been truly appalling, but Love had been brought to justice for his crimes. As Love was taken away, Mr Blackman's family members quietly hugged each other as they left the court.

Outside the court, Detective Superintendent Chantler welcomed the verdict, saying that Mark Love was not alone in committing the offences, and he would like to reassure members of the public that their investigations would continue to identify all of those who were yet to face justice.

Tuesday, 21st March 2017

Exactly a year after the brutal murder of Roy Blackman, the case remained open despite only two of the perpetrators being accounted for. The safe had not been found. Detective Chief Inspector Nick Gossett said that one person had been convicted of Mr Blackman's murder; however, they firmly believed that there were other people involved in the tragic incidents of that night, and they believed there were people who knew exactly who they were. Investigations to identify further suspects and recover the stolen property from Mr Blackman's home continued.

At the time of writing (2022), the remaining suspects had still not been apprehended, despite the number of arrests made in connection with the case, nor had the location of the safe been determined. From its dimensions, the weight of the safe could probably be estimated to weigh in the region of 300-500 kilograms. There would have been required a substantial amount of manpower, and expertise, to manoeuvre it from Roy Blackman's bungalow and into Love's van. This proves that there were considerably more individuals involved in the crime than just the two known suspects, but where are they now?

Sources

Websites

- www.ahbs.org.uk/news/ Ashford Hospital Broadcasting Service
- www.bbc.co.uk/news/uk-england
- www.cps.gov.uk/southeast/cps_southeast_news/
- www.dailymail.co.uk/
- www.findmypast.co.uk England & Wales, Births, 1837-2006, England & Wales marriages 1837-2005 and UK electoral registers, 2002-2014
- www.heart.co.uk/kent/news/
- www.itv.com/news/meridian/
- www.kentlive/news/kent-news/
- www.kentnews.co.uk/news/
- www.kentonline.co.uk
- www.kent.police.uk/news/appeals

- www.pressreader.com/uk/kentish-express-ashford-district/
- www.ryeandbattleobserver.co.uk/news/
- www.telegraph.co.uk/news/
- www.theguardian.com/uk-news/

Appendix A – Maps

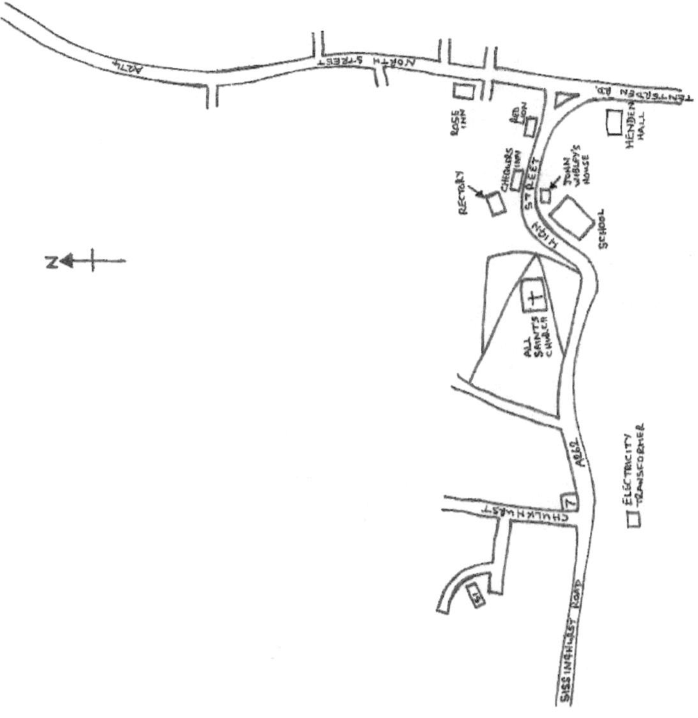

WEALDEN KENT

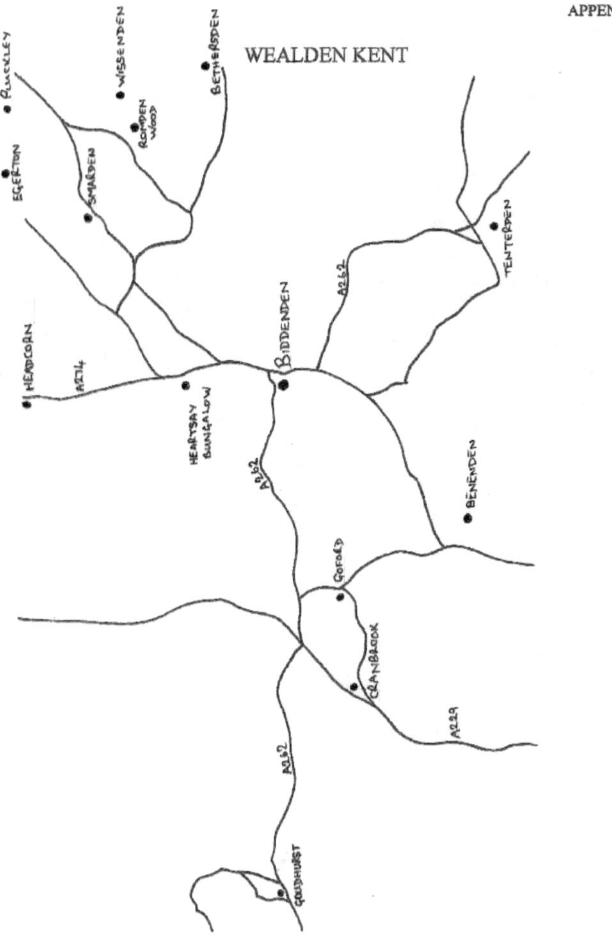

Appendix B – Bibliography

- Adams, E., 2014, *The Cranbrook Journal*, No. 25, A Victorian Anglican: William Peterson of Sissinghurst and Biddenden.

- Adams, E., 2015, *The Cranbrook Journal*, No. 26, The Biddenden Murder, 1899.

- Besant, w. & Rice. J., 1893, *The Golden Butterfly*, Chatto & Windus, London.

- Biddenden Local History Society, 2010, *Biddenden in Pictures*, YoubyYou Books, Biddenden Kent.

- Bishop, W., June 1991, *True Detective*, Kent Village Murder by the Rector's Daughter, Magazine Design & Publishing Ltd, Lancashire.

- Hills, C., 2020, *Buckingham Joe,* Austin Macauley Publishers, London.

- Joy, A. (Transcribed by*)*, 2009, *Burials in the Parish of Biddenden in the County of Kent - 1877-1992.*

- Kelly, E.R. (Ed.), 1882, *Kelly's Directory of Kent*, Kelly & Co., London.

- Odell, R., 2010, *The Mammoth Book of Bizarre Crimes*, Robinson.

- Pile, C.C.R., 1954, *Watermills and Windmills of Cranbrook*, Cranbrook & District Local History Society.

- *Bygone Kent*, The Long Blue Line - The Fowle Family's 165 Years of Police Service, Volume II, pp. 500-503.

- *Real Life Crimes*, Mind of Evil, Volume 8, Part 108, 1995, Eaglemoss Publications Ltd, London.
- *The Gentleman's Magazine*, Volume XLIII, p. 408-409, August 14 1773.
- *The Maiden Tribute* of *Modern Babylon*, reprinted from the *Pall Mall Gazette* of 6-10 July 1885, Pamphlet.
- *The Story of Biddenden*, published for the Biddenden Local History Society, 1996.

Appendix C – Acknowledgements

Are due to:

Dominic and Elena (in that sequence) who gave me the original idea and then the enthusiasm for documenting the murderous events associated with Biddenden;

Biddenden Post Office for supplying the local history publications necessary to appreciate the village of Biddenden and its history;

The *British Library*, London, for their friendly assistance in access to various historic and contemporary newspapers and for the use of their extensive repository on the *British Newspaper Archive* website;

The Kent Archives and Local History department of Kent County Council at Maidstone, for their help and support in the examination of a variety of old documents, particularly those of the eighteenth- and nineteenth-century quarter sessions.

www.ingramcontent.com/pod-product-compliance
Lightning Source LLC
Chambersburg PA
CBHW021323060726
47591CB00006B/1848